MW00450429

WISCONSIN SUPPER CLUB
Cookbook

WISCONSIN SUPPER CLUB
Cookbook

ICONIC FARE AND NOSTALGIA FROM LANDMARK EATERIES

MARY BERGIN

Globe
Pequot

GUILFORD, CONNECTICUT

All the information in this guidebook is subject to change. We recommend that you call ahead to obtain current information before traveling.

Reminder: Consuming raw or undercooked meats, poultry, seafood, shellfish, or eggs may increase your risk of food-borne illness.

Globe
Pequot

An imprint of Rowman & Littlefield
Distributed by NATIONAL BOOK NETWORK

Copyright © 2015 Mary Bergin

All photography is by the author unless otherwise noted in the Acknowledgments. Vintage photos are provided by supper club owners.

All rights reserved. No part of this book may be reproduced in any form or by any electronic or mechanical means, including information storage and retrieval systems, without written permission from the publisher, except by a reviewer who may quote passages in a review.

British Library Cataloguing in Publication Information Available

Library of Congress Cataloging-in-Publication Data
Bergin, Mary, 1955-
  Wisconsin supper club cookbook : iconic fare and nostalgia from landmark eateries / Mary Bergin.
    pages cm
  Includes index.
    ISBN 978-1-4930-0634-2 (pbk.) — ISBN 978-1-4930-1656-3 (ebook) 1. Cooking, American—Midwestern style. 2. Dinners and dining—Wisconsin. I. Title.
  TX715.2.M53B464 2015
  641.5977—dc23

                                                                    2015017366

∞™ The paper used in this publication meets the minimum requirements of American National Standard for Information Sciences—Permanence of Paper for Printed Library Materials, ANSI/NISO Z39.48-1992.

CONTENTS

Central Wisconsin   71

Southern Wisconsin   134

RECIPES BY COURSE

Salads

Entrees

On the Side

Desserts

FOREWORD: THE SUPPER CLUB IS A WISCONSIN ICON

It is a real pleasure to write the foreword for a book that features authentic and signature recipes from many of Wisconsin's legendary supper clubs. For people who have visited one of the supper clubs that submitted a recipe, the book will give them an opportunity to relive a pleasant memory. For people who have never dined in a supper club, reading this book might open a door to future "must-have" experiences.

There are supper clubs in other states, but it is hard to imagine a state that has more of this style of restaurant than Wisconsin. I would even venture to say that Wisconsin is the home of the supper club. Practically every rural town has a supper club that has been in existence for a long time and often is still being run by the family of the original owner. However, supper clubs abound in cities as well. They are just not quite as visible.

As chief executive of the Wisconsin Restaurant Association since 1981, I get many inquiries about restaurants in a particular area from people planning a visit to our great state. Most often they really want to know what a supper club is and where can they find one. I've come to the conclusion that the two things on most Wisconsin visitors' "to-do" lists are dine in a supper club and see Lambeau Field.

The recent resurgence of supper club popularity is easy to understand. For many it is nostalgia, a longing for a time past when life seemed simpler and went at a slower pace. In this era of technology and speed, people sometimes feel disconnected. Well, if a supper club is anything, it is connection. Supper clubs are known for being friendly and welcoming. Typically the owner is always there greeting customers, checking food, making drinks, and talking to people about their travels, family, and the news of the day.

Supper clubs have a lot of regular customers, and if you dine at one more than once, chances are "everybody knows your name." Historically, the supper club was the average person's answer, in a way, to the private dining clubs or country clubs.

Then, there is the food. Some menus have been retooled to be more modern, but the essence is still the same. Food is made from scratch and has the "homemade touch." Much of it is comfort food, the kind that makes your taste buds pop, your stomach warm, and the rest of you feel really good. Key recipes have often been in the family for years: Sometimes they are mom's, grandma's, and even great-grandma's secret recipe.

The drinks are generous and well made. While you can get a cold beer or a glass of wine, the cocktail is king at a supper club. The old-fashioned, Manhattan, gimlet, martini, Bloody Mary, and even the Tom Collins are often the drinks of choice. The bartender knows sports and everything else, including directions. Ask, and you won't get a blank look. You might get a story as well, but you will get directions.

Mary Bergin is an accomplished author and journalist whose specialties—travel and food—uniquely qualify her to write this book. I first became acquainted with Mary when she called on me for an occasional interview about restaurants and food. I always found her questions stimulating and her conclusions insightful. She didn't just get the answers to her questions and hang up; she was probing and we conversed. I began to think of Mary Bergin as an expert in dining, and we have commissioned her to write for our *Wisconsin Restaurateur* magazine. Those articles have included a feature on supper clubs, entitled "Old Fashioned Traditions and New Innovations," which was well-received by supper club owners and fans of the supper club, like myself.

The selection of supper clubs and recipes in this book gives you a taste of the romantic supper club tradition that is still going strong. While supper clubs are founded on tradition, there's room for innovation. Supper clubs are not stagnant or a throwback, they continue to modernize and augment traditional favorites to satisfy changing consumer preferences. Some of the newer supper clubs, in particular, are finding the perfect balance between the nostalgic and the contemporary.

Edward J. Lump, President and CEO
Wisconsin Restaurant Association

INTRODUCTION

I hear that you're looking for the ghost of Don Draper, or at least the old-fashioned that he ordered. Stiff drinks, thick chops, and sultry lounges were part of the retro *Mad Men* scene, but we've been living that dream for quite a while in Wisconsin. This is where supper clubs prosper and have long helped define our culture, although the vibe is not as brash, brazen, or intense as Madison Avenue apparently was in the 1960s.

What turns a restaurant into a supper club? That question is the bait for lots of banter within the Badger State, but out-of-staters inquire with genuine perplexity. They ask about club membership fees and whether vacationers are excluded. Restricted access has never been a part of the deal because, like a good tailgate at Lambeau, more means merrier.

The typical Wisconsin supper club doesn't take weekend reservations and has long waits for tables, but nobody cares. Downshift. Coast. Chill, why don't you? This is your destination for the night, not a hop between work and the theater. So talk among yourselves, engage strangers, flirt, eavesdrop, linger.

The backdrop for these reality shows varies, but in a perfect world supper clubs are:

- lit up by neon lights outside
- dimly lit inside
- open for dinner only
- loved by locals
- family owned, for generations
- better for couples than children
- overlooking a lake, woods, or farmland

The menu is predictable. Diners know what to expect and like it that way. This means supper clubs offer:

- huge portions
- doggie bags
- comfort foods
- from-scratch cooking
- longtime family recipes
- a relish tray at each table
- a fish fry on Friday
- prime rib on Saturday
- Bloody Marys on Sunday
- steaks and potatoes all week
- cocktails, especially brandy old-fashioneds, before dinner
- an ice-cream drink, especially grasshoppers, for dessert

What else? That question was posed at a museum's 2014 food history exhibit in Appleton, Wisconsin. My favorite responses, scrawled anonymously, were "marinated beets and suspenders" and "you can go back as an adult and feel the same as when you were a kid." Those answers are both expressions

of endearment and clues to the challenges accompanying the supper club stereotype.

Some people say supper clubs are dying in Wisconsin because they don't change. Others say the lack of change is their strength and distinction. I say it's always been rare for a supper club to fit a cookie-cutter definition, and that's a good thing. What we have today is a mix of culinary ingenuity, fluid business practices, and pride in upholding traditions, heritage, and community connections.

Supper clubs are where the Rotary Club meets. It's where your daughter's wedding reception is booked and post-funeral meals happen. The high school sports banquet is here, and it might be where your buddies gather for a weekly afternoon of sheepshead. You might propose marriage in a quiet nook or take a seat at the bar in your green and gold.

The hands-on approach and hard work of supper club owners appeal to blue-collar sensibilities but—like counter seating at a good diner—the mix of generations, income levels, and professions potentially benefits a wider swath of demographics. A good supper club operator who works the bar will smoothly divert his customers from talk about their differences in politics, religion, and lifestyle.

Supper clubs are changing, but that doesn't mean they are vanishing. Morphing is a better word. That means, despite the best efforts of anybody—including me—to be absolute when describing supper clubs, few fit the description perfectly. Each supper club is one of a kind, right down to what decorates the walls and shelves: mounted game animals, vintage family photos, or kitsch from bygone eras.

Many of these businesses began as simple stagecoach stops, roadhouses, or taverns that happened to sell food. They've already been through major revisions that added dance floors, other entertainment, banquet rooms, lunch, brunch, and more—or less—as dictated by changing times.

Throughout, customers stay loyal because the owner gets to know them by name, listens and responds to food or drink preferences, and, if working the kitchen, makes time for leisurely table-to-table visits. Even on hectic Saturday nights.

Our lack of agreement about what exactly constitutes a supper club "is why they are so vibrant today," suggests food historian Terese Allen of Madison, Wisconsin. "Any good folklorist will say this is what keeps the tradition alive and thriving."

Stricter drunk-driving laws, smoking bans, specialty diets, and changing dining trends all challenge supper club owners, especially those who base their prosperity on business as usual. Nearing extinction are printed matchbooks as a parting gift. A menu of hefty portions and many courses spells value only if it matches the average customer's appetite.

The evolution of food regulations plays a role, too: Automatically starting dinner with a tableside array of salads, pâtés, and other house-made nibbles—the traditional and complimentary relish tray—loses its charm as an investment when the supper club operator sees how much is left untouched. Food that used to be repurposed decades ago must be thrown away today. That makes the salad bar a more logical substitute for the relish tray.

All this talk, of course, is part of something bigger, humbling, and more complicated. University of Wisconsin researchers in 2014 turned the science behind supper club food into a well-attended evening of dissecting, sampling, and scrutinizing, as a part of the annual Wisconsin Science Festival. We got little lessons about the ten-thousand-year story of cheese and an introduction to *Saccharomyces cerevisiae*, the species of yeast that has played a key role in fermenting beer and other beverages throughout human history.

Geneticists with yellow, purple, orange, striped, and two-toned vegetables reminded us that carrots and beets aren't predictable monotones anymore. Add samples of saffron deviled eggs and spreads of orange dill butter: The possibilities for upheaval in traditions seem endless.

My cookbook research began with the compilation of a supper club database from myriad sources. I turned up at least 300 businesses, of which around 250 still are in operation, but keep hearing about others under my radar: They lack websites, aren't social media players, don't belong to a chamber of commerce, and don't advertise in traditional ways because their customers do a great job of spreading the word. A remarkable number of these supper clubs flourish in rural locations, miles from the nearest unincorporated town.

The forty supper clubs that are represented by one or more recipes in this cookbook show the huge spectrum of what exists in Wisconsin. They are a mix of rural and urban players, new businesses, and four-generation family endeavors, with modestly casual to flamboyant decor.

Their recipes are an amazing jumble of supper club classics and contemporary interpretations of supper club food. Complex entrees, decades-old family recipes, ethnic favorites, simple combinations, and practical ideas for busy cooks—all are here to provide both inspiration and simplification in the kitchen. All also are links to the very personal stories of how the supper club setting quietly continues to define the lives of many good people in Wisconsin.

Northern Wisconsin

We who live in Wisconsin routinely retreat "Up North" for a peaceful getaway, but the destination and boundaries are ambiguous. We've arrived when thick forests stretch beyond the horizon and the population of whitetail deer outnumbers people. A typical Northwoods county has fewer than 20,000 human inhabitants. Scarce is the four-lane highway, and two-lane routes may or may not be paved.

More than one-half of the state's fifteen thousand lakes are in Northern Wisconsin; they are a healthy habitat for walleye, muskie, and much more. Add whitefish from gorgeous but tempestuous Lake Superior.

Although people throughout Wisconsin embrace supper club dining, the culture is arguably strongest in the state's most rural confines. You could say the Northwoods is to supper clubs what Broadway is to theater; there are numerous good choices that hungry travelers find.

THE ABERDEEN

25 Twin Pines Road, Manitowish Waters
(715) 543-8700
aberdeenlodge.com
Owners: Larry and Gail Voss

A strong combination of sentimental attachment and perceived business potential motivated Larry and Gail Voss to open a restaurant and bar at The Aberdeen during the summer of 2014. They call it a supper club because of the menu, hours of business, and setting within the Manitowish Waters Chain of Lakes.

The operation is part of a complex with seven log cabins, each individually owned and in a forest of pines next to the Trout River, known for its excellent fishing. Gail's grandparents acquired land less than ten minutes away for hunting and fishing in the 1950s. They bought the sixty acres for five thousand dollars, sight unseen, because of a *Chicago Tribune* ad.

The family built a three-season hunting cabin with no electricity, an outhouse, and a water pump on the porch, Gail recalls. Her first visit was at age three, and as a teen she'd visit in summer while attending a private camp for girls and learning skills from water skiing to rifle handling. Now she and her husband talk about building a year-round home on the same property.

The Vosses are empty nesters "ready to do something different with our lives." Before moving to the Northwoods from northern Illinois, Gail returned to school to earn a law degree from Marquette University and has intentions to specialize in elder law, guardian work, and Native American tribal issues. Larry's finance experience—particularly in the buying, selling, and merger of manufacturing enterprises—adds another type of expertise to the business at hand. Another relative with a leading role is nephew Blake Borgstede, the general manager.

Their supper club, a red pine lodge constructed in 1995, sits on property that used to be a horse-riding area. A three-season porch seats forty diners, the main dining room has room for one hundred, and a roomy bar can hold another forty-five. A fourteen-foot-tall, double-sided fireplace separates the dining room and bar, where a sixty-inch TV hangs under a moose head. Several other animal mounts (from a taxidermist in nearby Boulder Junction) are showcased like local artwork, which also adorns the walls.

"We're trying to create a community space," Larry explains. "It's a place to come and relax, a meeting place for multiple generations," and one that welcomes customers who arrive by boat wearing casual attire. Previous owners closed the business in October, reopened in May, and operated fifteen pizza ovens. "That's what they were known for," Larry says, "but I think this building is too nice to be just a pizza place."

To succeed as a year-round supper club, Larry talks about how the business model needs to change after Labor Day because what tourists and local residents seek "is totally different." How people define "value" and choose to spend their money is often far different when on vacation versus day-to-day living at home.

In autumn, Thursday is Comfort Food Night, when entrees such as meat loaf or lasagna are lower-price specials. You're less likely to see this on a summer Thursday, but "everything is fluid here," Larry says. "We experiment a little and try to do historically successful things," which includes a fish fry on both Wednesday and Friday.

"When you get a feel for this place, it has a lot of character" but, that said, "you have to put a number to every transaction," and this factors into his calculated approach to supper club ownership.

Nephew Blake's goal in the kitchen is to "take Southern traditions and place them in a new light." That includes a cornmeal batter for fish, a proprietary seasoning blend for french fries, and coleslaw jazzed up with cayenne pepper, jalapeños, and hot sauce.

Blake Borgstede and head chef Allen Tassin share the credit for collaborating on this recipe. Instead of salt in the pico de gallo, they favor Cavender's blend of Greek seasonings.

GRILLED WALLEYE WITH ROASTED SHRIMP AND GARLIC PICO DE GALLO

For the pico de gallo:
¾ cup diced tomatoes
½ cup diced red onions
¼ cup chopped red bell pepper
⅛ cup cilantro, stems removed
½ tablespoon chopped jalapeño
   pepper, seeds removed
Salt to taste
1 teaspoon lemon juice
1 teaspoon lime juice

For the entree:
2 (8-ounce) walleye fillets
Salt, to taste
Pepper, to taste
1 teaspoon paprika
12 medium or large shrimp,
   peeled and deveined
¼ cup dry white wine
½ teaspoon chopped garlic
¼ cup butter
Chopped parsley, to garnish
Lemon wedges

Combine all pico de gallo ingredients in a bowl. Mix well and refrigerate.

Grill or poach the walleye for 5 to 8 minutes, seasoning with salt and pepper. Cook until fish no longer is translucent. Add paprika for color.

In separate pan, cook shrimp with white wine about 2 minutes, or until pink and firm. Add pico de gallo, garlic, and butter. Sauté 1 to 2 minutes, until heated through.

Place walleye on two plates. Add shrimp mixture. Garnish with parsley and lemon wedges. Serve with seasonal vegetables and wild rice.

SERVES 2

Wisconsin is home to eleven tribal nations that own and are the environmental stewards of at least five hundred thousand acres. Manitowish Waters is within sixty miles of two reservations: the Lac du Flambeau and Bad River Bands of Lake Superior Chippewa.

Native American Tourism of Wisconsin, a tribal consortium, keeps an online calendar of powwows and other events that are open to the public. Some gatherings distinguish one tribal culture from another. The largest is the annual Indian Summer Festival on Milwaukee's lakefront in early September; it involves dancing, re-created tribal villages, storytelling, a lacrosse tournament, and demos of traditional crafts. nativewisconsin.com, indiansummer .org, (414) 604-1000

CALDERWOOD LODGE SUPPER CLUB

1082 240th Avenue, Luck
(715) 472-2343
facebook.com/calderwoodlodge
Owner: Mike Thompson

"You're in Luck" is a billboard motto for a village of eleven hundred that loggers named in the 1800s; they felt in luck to travel as far as they did by sundown. The community on Big Butternut Lake is seventy miles northeast of the Twin Cities, so you're likely to find fans of the Minnesota Vikings and Twins, plus an occasional retiree of the sports teams in the area.

Stately and stoic Calderwood Lodge is almost ten miles southwest of Luck. The fieldstone building is flanked by farmland and on the shore of narrow Bone Lake, about six miles long and known for its muskie fishing. "The crappies and sunnies don't get a chance to get big here," executive chef Paul Howland says, because they get eaten by larger species. The lake also was the site of a long-ago battle between Chippewa and Sioux tribes.

Boats that cut across the lake in summer are replaced by snowmobiles in winter. The wealthy quietly retreat here, but Amish and Mennonite families

also are in the rural neighborhood. During its heyday, Paul says, the restaurant would serve one hundred guests per day, every day. Now dining hours are shorter—from 4 to 9 p.m. on New Year's Eve, for example—but there is a resurgence of from-scratch cooking. That means pan-reduction sauces for steaks and a wine-cream base for Alfredo sauce, "not just heating a bag of it, premade."

The chef's biggest challenge? "Fine dining has lost a lot of its command in the marketplace," he says. A staff of five, none related, operate the entire supper club and find ways to gain attention in unusual ways. In the bar and entrance area are many stuffed animals that are battery powered, and a life-size dummy named Ernie is voice activated.

The Calderwood was built from 1918 to 1922 as a family retreat, using neighborhood stone and lumber. The task was not easy. Charles Calder, who owned 720 acres along Bone Lake, used horses to drag tree trunks through the woods, and some of these logs are still ceiling joists. From the 1920s until the Great Depression, the destination was a spa for the wealthy; they traveled by train to Luck from as far as Illinois and Iowa. The allure was a natural spring that contained lithium; guests would fill containers and take home the water because of its purported medicinal value.

CALDERWOOD 1992

Clean cottages with screened porches were for rent. "This is not a fashionable resort, so leave your good clothes at home," promotional materials advised. "We set a generous, wholesome table, with fresh vegetables and good country meals, also plenty of milk and cream." The rate, with meals, was $3.50 per day for a solo traveler.

Today the renovated building totes the line between Old World comfort and eccentric antics. "This place just screams 'haunted house'" because of the dim lighting, Paul notes, and it turns into a fun Halloween destination. The 2014 party was the Calderwood's thirty-fifth. Kids arrive early, with parents, and later it's adults only at the bar with "Rocky," a bartender whose work here began in 1986. Paul is the newcomer whose work here began in 2014.

The lodge wasn't a supper club until the 1980s. Before that it was a beer bar and dance hall with rumors in the 1930s that a house of ill repute was operating upstairs. Overflow dining is accommodated in this part of the building today.

The area has a gangster history, too, but no dramatic evidence of it, so look for the stick-on bullet holes that are strategically placed at the bar and elsewhere. Local residents swap stories about how Al Capone, John Dillinger, and Ma Barker were among the mobsters who sought a quiet and private respite at the Calderwood.

Luck was home to Duncan Yo-Yo Company from 1946 to 1965 and considered itself the Yo-Yo Capital of the World, because so many of the toys were produced with locally harvested maple trees. Many families in the village worked for the company, and peak production hit thirty-six hundred yo-yos per hour. By 1962 there reportedly were more yo-yos than children in the United States.

The company hired yo-yo operators to tour the world and show children how to perform tricks with the spinning toy, but changes in technology and terminology eventually worked against Duncan. By the time bankruptcy was filed in 1965, less-expensive yo-yos made of plastic were gaining popularity. A court ruling that Duncan no longer could claim the word yo-yo as a trademark meant that other manufacturers of the toy could advertise and market it that way.

Paul Howland adds thyme in this glaze as "a wonderful wake-up, background flavor that makes it more fun to swallow." He suggests serving the entree on a bed of mixed greens drizzled with vinaigrette (he favors a peppercorn-Champagne combination in the dressing).

GLAZED SALMON

For the salmon:

4 (8-ounce) salmon fillets

2–4 tablespoons melted butter

Salt and pepper, to taste

For the glaze:

2 ounces Amaretto

1 ounce Cointreau

2 tablespoons apricot preserves

½ teaspoon thyme

Baste salmon fillets with melted butter. Add salt and pepper. Broil 8 to 10 minutes, depending on fillet thickness, until temperature at center is 125°F.

While fish is broiling, combine Amaretto, Cointreau, and apricot preserves in a small saucepan over low heat. Stir in thyme. Add glaze to top of fillets and serve.

SERVES 4

THE CHIPPEWA INN

9702 N. Highway B, Hayward
(715) 462-3648
chippewainnsupperclub.com
Owners: Tom and Debbie Landgraf

Before The Chippewa Inn, there was De Shanty on this rural Northwoods property, just a tavern for the neighborhood after the lifting of Prohibition. Although the address is Hayward, the supper club is fifteen miles east of the city, at the edge of Chequamegon National Forest and the Chippewa Flowage. By 1946, new owners Richard and Centa Eckart were eyeing a dance hall across the road that was for sale; they bought it, moved it, attached it to the bar, converted part into a dining room, and opened Dick's Chippewa Inn.

The next round of owners, Anna and Otto Willems, added an authentic German flair to the menu and enlarged the restaurant. They were former bakery owners in Chicago, and a son-in-law was a headwaiter in Germany before working at Chicago's best-known German-American restaurant, The Berghoff.

Several German specialties—pork shank with sauerkraut to apple strudel—remain popular at "The Chip" today, and the Landgrafs added a reputation for

excellence in steaks after assuming ownership in 1995. Their Kansas City steaks are dry-aged for twenty-eight days.

German recipes were included in the property transaction, and schnitzels remain a top seller, followed by walleye and rib eye dinners. One page of the menu is for Bavarian fare; the sauerbraten is made with beef brisket, producing a rich gravy that is good for dunking dumplings to bread. "Schnitzel of the Month" specials have included Schnitzel Berliner: breaded pork with sautéed onions, peppers, and mozzarella cheese.

Count The Chip among the dwindling number of supper clubs that still automatically deliver an extensive relish tray to diners. On it are marinated olives, port wine cheese spread, pickled herring, liver pâté, cherry peppers, and raw veggies. Sauerkraut and creamed cucumbers also used to be a part of the mix.

Debbie Landgraf says she and her husband moved from Chicago to Hayward with their children because "we wanted to get the kids out of the

city" after selling a family business. They got acquainted with the Hayward area while visiting friends who have a cabin on a nearby lake. "My husband wanted a restaurant, and this one was for sale," she explains.

Son Eric does the cooking, "building flavors slowly—he doesn't rush it." That includes using wine instead of stock to enrich the flavor of his goulash. The chef says he used to experiment with "Sundays Around with World" menu specials, presenting entrees from lesser-known cuisines, such as Portugal, but decided it's more practical to stick with tried-and-true offerings. Devoting each Sunday to a different country was time-consuming, and it was sometimes hard to modify recipes for restaurant-size quantities.

Live music is part of the Saturday night menu, thanks to a local piano player and husband–wife duo who perform jazz and pop on sax, clarinet, flute, and/or violin. What else makes The Chip different from most? In display cases are dolls and dollhouses that Debbie's mother made long ago for granddaughter Amanda, who turned twenty-eight in 2014.

*Eric Landgraf learned his craft at culinary schools in Italy and France. The family sh[...]
recipes, including this longtime favorite on the relish tray that each customer receives.*

MARINATED OLIVES

Drain juice from the jar of olives. Mix remaining ingredients in a bowl and pour into the jar of olives. Rotate "every now and then" to marinate the olives.

MAKES 1 POUND

1 (16-ounce) jar green olives
¼ cup olive oil
1 tablespoon balsamic vinegar
2 cloves garlic, minced
1 teaspoon sugar
½ teaspoon dried oregano
½ teaspoon dried basil
⅛ teaspoon red pepper flakes
Pepper to taste

Frozen, shredded hash browns that are thawed in the refrigerator shorten the preparation time for this popular side dish, which is served with a choice of applesauce, maple syrup, or sour cream.

POTATO PANCAKES

4 large eggs

1 teaspoon salt

¼ teaspoon white pepper

¼ teaspoon nutmeg

1 (16-ounce) package frozen
   hash browns, thawed

½ cup flour

¼ cup chopped parsley

Vegetable oil, as needed

Blend eggs, salt, white pepper, and nutmeg. Place hash browns in a large bowl and add egg mixture. Combine well with hands. Move hash browns into a food processor, one small batch at a time, and blend again. Mix flour and parsley into the batter.

Pour vegetable oil into a frying pan to ½-inch deep and heat to medium heat. Drop ⅓ cup of batter per pancake, flattening slightly with a large spoon as you go. Cook over medium heat until brown and crisp. Flip and brown the other side. Drain on paper towels and keep warm in oven.

SERVES 4–6

This alternative to the traditional Thanksgiving pumpkin pie provides a refreshing twist to th[e] *iar flavors that we crave during autumn.*

PUMPKIN CHEESECAKE

Preheat oven to 350°F. Mix crust ingredients together and press into a 10-inch springform pan. Set aside.

For the filling, combine the cream cheese, pumpkin, and vanilla with an electric mixer. In a separate bowl combine the sugar, cinnamon, nutmeg, and cloves. Add this mixture to the cream cheese mixture and blend until smooth. Add eggs and mix well.

Pour the filling into prepared crust. Bake 35 to 40 minutes. Remove from oven and let rest 5 minutes.

Mix topping ingredients and pour over cheesecake. Return to oven and bake an additional 5 minutes. Cool on a wire rack. Cover and refrigerate overnight before serving.

SERVES 8–12

For the crust:
1½ cups crushed graham crackers
½ cup sugar
¼ cup melted butter

For the filling:
2 (8-ounce) packages cream cheese, softened
½ cup pumpkin puree
½ teaspoon vanilla
½ cup sugar
½ teaspoon cinnamon
¼ teaspoon nutmeg
Dash of ground cloves
2 large eggs

For the topping:
1 (8-ounce) container sour cream
¾ cup sugar
1 teaspoon vanilla

Five miles north of the Chippewa Inn is North Star Homestead Farms, a 1919 farm with a cafe, market, and creamery operated by a trio of women, Ann Berlage and daughters Laura and Kara.

Key ingredients for meals come from the family's aquaponics greenhouse, where kohlrabi to tilapia grow. From the farm's sheep come meat for gyros, a breakfast lamb sausage, and gelato made with sheep's milk. Other small-scale farms provide blueberries to beef for the menu and market, which also sells locally made artwork, jewelry, music, and items using recycled materials. northstarhomestead.com, (715) 462-3453

Jake's Supper Club on Tainter Lake

E5690 Highway D, Menomonie
(715) 235-2465
jakessupperclub.com
Owners: Kim and Peter Gruetzmacher

Peter Gruetzmacher knew of Jake's as a college student, when "Ham and Jam" on Thursday night helped feed and entertain him and classmates at the University of Wisconsin–Stout, a ten-minute drive south. The native of Minnesota's Twin Cities was studying restaurant management at the Menomonie campus. Free ham sandwiches and music outdoors were the bait that drew college kids, golfers, and others to the remote supper club with the big deck and tiki bar on Tainter Lake.

A "For Sale" sign at Jake's would be the enticement that Peter needed to return after graduation. He was employed at a restaurant in Minneapolis and fishing for muskie in Wisconsin with his father, Kim, when they heard the news in 2008. They took a detour home, took a good look at the supper club, and decided it would be a great place to become their own boss.

"It was a big step," Peter acknowledges, and with the purchase of the property came substantial investments to replace or update the roof, furnace,

Jake's Supper Club on Tainter Lake   **21**

fireplaces, kitchen, and other infrastructure. Now customers are back to pulling up their boats to Jake's dock during summer, especially for the live music that follows brunch on Sunday afternoon.

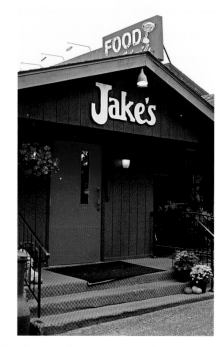

When Jake's resumed business in 2009, locals expressed their gratitude to the new owners. To out-of-towners this might be just a place to linger in warm weather, but to year-round lakeshore residents the shuttered business was a significant community loss. Jake's was "a landmark meeting place," Peter says, and the reason some customers chose to live on the murky, sixteen-thousand-acre fishing lake that is known for its walleye, crappie, and northern pike.

The property was a bait shop and gas station in the 1940s, then a convenience store. A bar was added before a full kitchen. When known as Doug and Mary's River's Edge Resort in the 1970s, a few cabins were for rent; now only one remains. The waterfront restaurant is so remote that deer, wild turkey, and an occasional black bear are part of the neighborhood.

Peter gives Jake Frank—"the consummate restaurateur"—credit for expanding the menu and making it a special-occasion destination, long billed as where "prime rib is king." He expanded to dining room size and "turned it from less of a bar and more of a supper club" by the early 1980s. Son-in-law John Lynch took over in 1992, but a tight economy and hike in competition took a toll on the business.

Making sure food quality is top-notch is a priority for the Gruetzmachers, but so is service and atmosphere. "Anybody can pour a beer," Peter observes. The tiki bar remains a hot spot during summer, when it stays open until midnight. Inside, prime rib remains the signature entree; it is slow roasted overnight and seasoned with a spice blend that includes rosemary. The record for present ownership is sixteen logs of beef served in a day; each weighs in at fourteen to twenty pounds.

What else? At least two dozen local boat owners bring out the red, white, and blue for the annual boat parade on the Fourth of July. Besides decorating pontoons and themselves, boaters use water guns to splash spectators and throw candy to the kids. The flotilla traditionally ends up docked at Jake's afterward.

Prime rib vegetable soup is on the menu every day at Jake's, and other soups rotate through the menu. This creamy, hearty soup is especially popular during winter and is sometimes part of the Sunday buffet. To make the soup's thickener (roux), melt 1 cup butter over medium heat and whisk in 1¼ cups flour. Roux left over from this recipe can be refrigerated for use another time.

CHICKEN WILD RICE SOUP

Melt butter in a stockpot over medium heat. Add carrots, onions, and celery. Sauté until soft. Don't brown. Stir in sherry, chicken base, basil, white pepper, and thyme. Cook 8 to 10 minutes. Add water, cream, and milk. Bring to a near boil.

Whisk in roux. When incorporated, add chicken. Simmer until thickened, 20 to 30 minutes. Stir in rice and cook 5 more minutes. Serve.

SERVES 6–10

1½ teaspoons butter
½ cup diced carrots
½ cup diced white onions
½ cup diced celery
⅓ cup dry sherry
¼ cup chicken base
1½ teaspoons basil
1 teaspoon white pepper
½ teaspoon thyme
2¾ cups water
2 cups heavy cream
1⅓ cups milk
¼ cup roux (see note, above)
2½ cups diced cooked chicken
1½ cups cooked wild rice

Peter Gruetzmacher developed this recipe and rotates it through the year with other chicken entrees on the supper club menu.

ARTICHOKE CHICKEN

2 tablespoons clarified butter

Flour, as needed

Salt and pepper, to taste

6 (4-ounce) chicken fillets

¼ cup white wine

¼ cup heavy whipping cream

12–15 capers

3 oven-roasted Roma tomatoes,
 sliced in half

¼ teaspoon sugar

1 (14-ounce) can artichoke
 hearts

1 tablespoon cold unsalted
 butter

Heat clarified butter in a frying pan. Blend flour, salt, and pepper in a bowl. Dredge chicken in the seasoned flour. Place the chicken in the pan over medium heat. When browned (6 to 8 minutes), turn over. Add wine, cream, capers, tomatoes, and sugar. Simmer until reduced by half.

Add drained artichokes. Cook until heated through. Add butter and stir to incorporate. Top chicken with artichoke sauce when plating the entree.

SERVES 3

One of the world's largest college degree programs in hospitality management is a ten-minute drive from Tainter Lake. The University of Wisconsin–Stout provides instruction in hotel, restaurant, and tourism management. The school also has hospitality study-abroad programs in Spain, Australia, and the Netherlands.

A newer offering is a thirty-credit and ten-course master's degree program in hospitality strategy for established managers in the industry. "UW–Stout is known nationally and around the world for producing top-notch employees in the hospitality and tourism industry," notes Chancellor Bob Meyer. "This new program will elevate our status and help the industry find the leaders it needs to compete in the twenty-first century." uwstout.edu, (715) 232-2567

Lehman's Supper Club

2911 South Main Street, Rice Lake
(715) 234-9911
lehmanssupperclub.com
Owners: Harold "Butch" and Trudy Lehman

If you want to get a rise out of a newcomer to Lehman's, rave about the Rock Potato. No competitor serves anything quite like it. The tater is dressed up with cheese sauce or sour cream and is the foundation for an unforgettable dining experience. Farmers near Rice Lake harvest many potatoes, but this breed is no match for the others because it's an actual stone, the size and shape of a spud.

Rock Potato presentations and special orders for Bugs on Food are among Butch Lehman's little jokes. He also kids about occasionally dropping his pants in the kitchen, to ease staff tension on a busy night, "but I always have my apron on."

Butch and wife Trudy are the kitchen expeditors, taking the lead on grilling to plate setup with the help of others at four or five food stations. The Lehmans met during high school and are proof that some couples can work side-by-side and survive. "You try to keep it light and lively," he says. It's convenient that they get along so well as chief cook and bottle washers because "if you're in this business, you're pretty much married to it."

Four generations of the family have kept Lehman's in operation since it opened in the early 1930s as a bar with dancing and lunches of standard fare, like hot roast beef sandwiches and chicken noodle soup. Paul Lehman called it the Hi-Way Inn back then, as it was one mile out of town and on his Red Cedar Farm. "Come early," promotional materials implored. "When you must leave, hurry back."

Treats at the modern-day Lehman's include hot and light popovers, baked on select nights, and a french onion au gratin soup that draws raves. Grandma's Red Cedar Farm Chicken Dinner, served family style, is a longtime Sunday special. It starts with chicken dumpling soup and ends with an array of dessert choices. Butch says his grandmother used to serve the meal to farm crews before machinery made it possible for farmers to harvest crops without the help of their neighbors. From-scratch recipes for this meal and many others are in the Lehman family cookbook, "tattered and torn but still readable."

Count on Butch to retreat from the kitchen to dining room, even on busy nights, to banter with guests and ask how they like their meals. He was an only child whose first memories of the business are surprises that his parents would bring home: a burger and fries, a chicken basket, a dessert. He was a sociology major who returned home during his second year of college because of his dad's lung cancer surgery. That was shortly before Christmas, and Butch decided not return to school.

One of the Lehmans' goals for their five children is to help all of them earn a college degree. As of 2014 three had graduated and two were still students. The deal is that the parents and student each pay half of the cost. "We tell them they can pay their half by working at the supper club, if they want, but we also want them to be aware of what else is out there in the world."

Butch says there's a lot for teens to learn from restaurant work, and it's not all about food. "Interacting with customers and employees is important and getting harder for kids today" because of texting and computers. "Our kids have learned how to meet, greet, and talk with other people."

Son John chose to return to Rice Lake and Lehman's after college graduation, which pleases his parents, and he's leading the supper club into the world of websites, social media, and contemporary point-of-sales systems. When the family got word that a second grandchild was on the way, Trudy quipped that it was time for Butch to grow up. He's not sure if he agrees and says life is good.

"It's more than a business," Butch concludes. "So many repeat customers are third and fourth generations of families. It's amazing how tight that bond is for us, and it's fun. What's the saying? Like what you do and do what you like—we give it our best shot on a daily basis. That's true of many supper clubs and small businesses, but we really mean that, from the heart."

Lehman's serves about thirty types of house-made soup per month, and the cycle includes this favorite. Don't believe Butch when he deadpans that it was designed as a way to use up wilted lettuce.

BLT SOUP

1 pound bacon
½ cup butter
1¼ cups flour
3½ quarts chicken stock
6 diced Roma tomatoes
¼ teaspoon nutmeg
⅛ teaspoon cayenne pepper
1 quart warmed heavy cream
1 head iceberg lettuce,
  shredded
Salt and pepper, to taste
Toasted croutons

Dice bacon strips and brown in a stockpot. Remove meat, cool, crumble, and set aside.

Add butter to bacon fat in the stockpot and melt. Whisk in flour. Cook and stir 2 to 3 minutes over low heat. Add chicken stock and blend.

Next into the stockpot are the tomatoes, nutmeg, and cayenne pepper. Blend and bring to a low boil. After 5 minutes, add warmed cream, lettuce, and crumbled bacon. Bring to a simmer, season to taste, and serve, garnishing with croutons.

MAKES 1½ GALLONS

Only Idaho and Washington produce more potatoes than Wisconsin, whose estimated 140 growers are responsible for the ranking. Most of them farm in the sandy parts of central Wisconsin because potatoes require well-drained soil, and much of the crop is irrigated.

Wisconsin leads the nation in cranberry production, harvesting about 60 percent of the US crop in the upper two thirds of the state. The three-day Warrens Cranberry Festival, held during the last full weekend of September, is the world's largest festival for the berry. It happens in a village of 400 residents and draws 120,000 visitors. Business as usual means tours of cranberry bogs, cranberries in all courses of food, and three miles of craft, food, and flea market vendors. cranfest.com, (608) 378-4200

Maiden Lake Supper Club

15649 Maiden Lake Road, Mountain
(715) 276-6479
maidenlakesupperclub.com
Owners: M. J. and Trina Dinkelman

Wisconsin is blessed with three water-rich borders because of Lake Michigan, Lake Superior, the Mississippi River, and St. Croix River. Add around fifteen thousand inland lakes, and it's no wonder the Friday fish fry turned into a long-standing, statewide cultural institution.

This is true at 278-acre Maiden Lake, too, where freshwater perch from Lake Erie, Atlantic cod, and walleye pike from the Canadian side of Lake Superior feed hundreds on a Friday night. Expect a two-hour wait for seating during summer. Walleye pike is the most popular fish choice, and the Maiden Lake Combo—walleye and scallops—is among the pricier entrees.

A fish fry also is available on Tuesday during summer "for people who don't want to fight the Friday crowd," says Trina Dinkelman. In 2003 she and her husband bought Maiden Lake Supper Club from her in-laws, Mike and Georgia Dinkelman, who operated the place for twenty-five years.

Mike, a former captain at the South Milwaukee Fire Department, still keeps his hands in the supper club business, literally. He pin-bones all the walleye, around two tons of it every year. It is tedious work that involves the removal of a middle flap from each fillet.

Fish lovers have their choice of eating fillets that are broiled, beer battered, or coated with seasoned flour. Trina is the main cook and learned the trade from her father-in-law. The mom of two sons also has experience as a waitress, hostess, and bartender.

She and M. J. have learned where to experiment as supper club owners and which items are sacred. In the latter category are generous portions and prime rib on Saturday; the supply has been known to sell out by 6 p.m. "Around here, you have to stick with tradition—people expect it," Trina says. "We do try to invite certain changes," like adding wines and martini choices, lighter-fare options, and more pasta and chicken dishes.

The couple also manages ten condo units, some of which are rented by the week to vacationers. The getaways replace the little cabins of Maiden Lake Resort that used to line the lake, and Trina has seen the waterfront gain affluence in another way: "Some of those lake cottages . . . my house would fit in their garage."

Although the lake has no public beach, there is a public boat landing and occasionally seaplanes in the neighborhood. "So they come by land, sea, and air to eat here," she says. A three-level deck that overlooks Maiden Lake was added in 1985, and it's a popular gathering place.

The mailing address is Mountain, but Lakewood is only one mile away. Both are small communities (the population of each hovers around eight hundred), and their year-round recreational trails venture into Chequamegon–Nicolet National Forest.

The supper club is always closed on one weekday per week in summer—"that's family time," Trina says. "We were never getting any time together as a family." So now they are able to enjoy more than the view from their lakefront business and adjacent home during the prime time of the year.

In Jenny June's *American Cookery Book*, a regional cookbook published in 1870, is an abundance of fish recipes, including two for "Lake Superior Style" whitefish that are boiled and broiled. The author described whitefish as "the most delicious of lake fish." Her fish recipes often called for the fillets to be dredged with flour and fried.

The Great Lakes yield far more varieties of fish than this, but invasive species, mercury levels, and overfishing have taken a toll on the commercial fishing industry. That means the average fish fry uses fillets from other parts of the nation or world.

The University of Wisconsin Sea Grant Institute keeps tabs on how Great Lakes fish populations and environments change and promotes eating fish caught sustainably and locally. Research, education, and outreach are key program components. eatwisconsinfish.org, (608) 262-0905

Trina Dinkelman's beer batter coats perch and cod as they are ordered on Friday and Tuesday nights at her supper club. She prefers to use a darker beer, and the exact amount of beer to use depends upon the desired thickness of coating.

One batch of the batter she makes is four times as much as the recipe below makes, and this smaller yield is still enough to coat six-ounce portions of fish for at least one dozen people. Trina says leftover batter can be frozen and used another time; just thaw overnight in the refrigerator.

BEER BATTERED FISH

4½ cups flour

1 egg

½ teaspoon salt

½ teaspoon baking powder

1–2 (12-ounce) bottles beer

Cooking oil, as needed

4½ pounds perch or cod fillets

Mix flour, egg, salt, baking powder, and beer until thoroughly blended and no longer lumpy.

Heat cooking oil in a deep fryer or frying pan. Dip fish fillets into batter, one by one, and drop carefully into fryer until golden brown, 4 to 5 minutes. Turn, if necessary, to brown evenly. Drain and serve.

SERVES 12

maxsells Restaurant

209 Central Avenue, Florence
(715) 528-5511
facebook.com/maxsellsrestaurant
Owners: Donald and Rachel Egelseer

A mere forty-four hundred people live in Florence County; only one of Wisconsin's seventy-two counties (Menominee) is home to fewer people. Florence County is on the Wisconsin–Michigan border, about 80 percent of the 495 square miles is forest and none of the communities are incorporated.

About twenty-three hundred people live in Florence, the county seat, and the area is best known for hunting, fishing, silent sports, snowmobiling, and ATV riding. Life can be rugged, winters harsh, and employment opportunities lean in this northeastern part of the state.

Such a backdrop makes Maxsells all the more unusual. The supper club operates from an elegant three-story Prairie School–style house that was added to the National Register of Historic Places in 2014. Daily specials are a mix of

what you'd expect from a supper club (fish on Friday, prime rib on Saturday), plus ethnic surprises like chicken piccata on Thursday or wiener schnitzel on Wednesday.

The house was built in 1899 for lumber baron David Fulmer and later became the home of Max Sells, Florence County's first district attorney. Numerous other people called this place home before the Egelseers bought it in 2000 and began a ground-up renovation that lasted six years. The building's foundation crumbled shortly after work began. "Maybe it just should have been demolished," Rachel Egelseer acknowledges, but she also saw potential and faded beauty. It was not the first Florence structure that she and her husband decided was worth saving. Think more like one of a dozen.

The couple bought a lake home getaway in the area during the 1980s and otherwise lived about two hundred miles south. They operated an auto recycling business for thirty-five years, until selling it in 1998 and becoming year-round Northwoods residents. What started as semiretirement turned into their revitalization of Florence, one building at a time.

So now the Judge House, a yellow Victorian across the street from Maxsells, is a cultural events center and office space. Encore on Central Ballroom, the former town hall, is home to fitness studios and banquet space. Other enterprises include an antiques store and the restored Carriage House that is booked for wedding receptions The work continues, and Florence is changing from a tired to touristy little town.

"These buildings were being put up for sale, and nobody was buying them," Rachel explains. "It's nice to see these places used again, instead of being eyesores" because of disrepair.

Downstairs dining is what anchors the nearly five-thousand-square-foot Maxsells, which was on the edge of town when built but now is smack downtown. Loyal customers and visitors mix in the fifty-two-seat dining area, which includes an enclosed forty-foot-long porch that overlooks fifty-acre Fisher Lake and its public beach. Upstairs is public lodging, and among the five choices is a suite whose private patio faces the lake.

Overnight rates include breakfast, but not at Maxsells. What guests get is a certificate to order what they want at one of two other Florence eateries. "That gives them a taste of local flavor while helping out these other places," says Rachel, who was voted Citizen of the Year in Florence in 2010 because of her work to rejuvenate the town.

Former Executive Chef David Knickelbein insisted on using "silver dollar mushrooms," each around three inches in diameter, for this recipe. He would purchase them through a wholesale distributor, and each mushroom cap overflows with the healthful stuffing. When making this appetizer with large button mushrooms from the average grocery store, the yield is closer to two dozen.

SPINACH-STUFFED MUSHROOMS

Preheat oven to 400°F. Remove mushroom stems. Place mushroom caps on a baking sheet and drizzle with ¼ cup olive oil. Sprinkle with salt and pepper, to taste. Bake 12 minutes. Remove from oven and cool.

Coat a 12-inch stainless steel frying pan with ¼ cup olive oil. Over medium heat, add spinach, garlic, and salt and pepper to taste. Cook until spinach wilts. Add wine and deglaze pan.

Cool wilted spinach to room temperature. Add cheese and bread crumbs. Combine thoroughly.

Stuff mushroom caps with spinach mixture. Warm in 400°F oven for 8 to 10 minutes. Serve.

MAKES 6

6 large mushrooms
½ cup extra virgin olive oil, divided
Salt and pepper, to taste
1 pound fresh baby spinach
2 tablespoons chopped fresh garlic cloves
¼ cup dry white wine
¼ cup grated Parmigiana Reggiano cheese
¼ cup coarsely ground bread crumbs

MR. G'S LOGAN CREEK GRILLE

5890 Highway 57, Jacksonport
(920) 823-2112
mrgslogancreekgrille.com
Owners: Bob and Mary Geitner

The Door County peninsula is Wisconsin's version of Cape Cod, and the area is among the state's most frequented tourist destinations. It is the thumb on our mitten-shaped state, abundant in parks, shoreline, and waterfront views—so much water on three sides that inland lakes tend to get ignored.

Veer east to explore Door County's quieter side, along rugged Lake Michigan, known for its jagged cliffs and bogs much more than groomed golf courses and balmy beaches. Near the edge of Logan Creek State Natural Area and ecologically rich and diverse Clark Lake is Mr. G's, operated by the same family since 1973.

The former Fernwood Gardens was built in 1932 by Alfred and Anna Gabler; he was an orchestra leader and their ballroom was known as the county's largest dance pavilion. The adjoining Fernwood Club served food. Changes in ownership, a fire in 1950 that destroyed the ballroom, and a name change to the Pal-Dora in the 1960s all made for precarious times. The ballroom, although rebuilt, eventually deteriorated.

By the time Bob and Lorraine Geitner bought the business in 1973, they already had two decades of supper club ownership elsewhere in the county. Son Bob Jr. worked at Mr. G's from the start and in 1981 assumed ownership with his wife, Mary. The couple raised five children above the restaurant, and each has worked at the supper club during some part of their life. "One bathroom and two bedrooms for the kids," notes Mary. "It was a great time for our family with lots of memories, most of them pretty funny."

There was no running upstairs after 5 p.m., because that could be heard in the dining room. "No showers, only baths," Mary says. "Once the dishwasher was going in the kitchen, there wasn't enough water pressure to take a shower." She was a special education teacher when they bought the restaurant, and gives her mother-in-law credit for teaching her how to cook for a crowd. "Lorraine was one of those unique people who could make a dinner out of anything she had in the refrigerator," Mary says. "It was very new to me."

Tender, fall-off-the-bone ribs, which win local Rib Fest competitions, are the top-selling entree. They arrive with a traditional barbecue sauce and a sauce made with Door County cherries. A popular appetizer is fried cheese curds that begin with squeaky chunks from Renard's Cheese, made twenty miles southwest. And although Mr. G's no longer delivers a tableside relish tray to diners, Mary sometimes adds her liver pâté to the barroom hors d'oeuvres table of cheese and crackers, salsa and chips.

"My favorite dessert to serve is my homemade Buttered Rum Banana Pecan Pie," she says. "The caramel and bananas along with the dark rum and loads of pecans make it a dessert worth taking home part of your dinner for, so you have room for it. It's that good."

Customers are a mix of year-round residents and curious tourists, which means the Geitners probably explain supper club basics more often than colleagues in other parts of the state. A common question from out-of-staters is, "What's an old-fashioned?" Unlike many other Door County dining spots, Mr. G's stays open all year, and some staffers have worked there more than thirty years. Seating in the sunroom is a draw in summer, and the wood-burning fireplace adds coziness in winter.

"We serve excellent food without all the tourist prices," Mary says. "We are here not only for the tourist trade, but also for our local customers. We hope to meet the people who dine with us and keep them as return customers."

Their children—Matthew, Mark, Robert, Sarah, and Chris—are all adults now but still show up to work in some capacity during the year, "whether it's to bartend for a big event, wait on tables, or just to give advice on remodeling and running events," their mother says. "It's good to have young eyes taking a second look at what we've built over the years."

"Even though people might think they don't like cabbage, when this soup is served, it surprises everyone because it seriously doesn't taste like cabbage at all," Mary Geitner promises. "Customers love when I serve this at my restaurant."

FRENCH CABBAGE SOUP

Melt butter in a stockpot and add flour. Blend and cook for 1 minute. Set aside.

Boil onions, carrots, and potatoes until soft. Drain. Set aside.

Bring chicken broth to a boil. Add cabbage and cook until cabbage is soft. Add the butter–flour mixture, and cook until thick. Add vegetables and sausage. Warm through.

MAKES 1 GALLON

8 tablespoons butter
1 cup flour
¾ cup chopped onions
3½ cups chopped carrots
3 cups cubed potatoes
3 quarts chicken broth
3 cups chopped fresh cabbage
8 ounces cooked kielbasa or
  Polish sausage, cubed

"I often find myself making an extra kettle of the vegetables because I love a nice, thick soup," Mary says of this recipe. *"If you like the taste of beer, you can add more as long as it doesn't thin it out too much."* She says two or three cans of cheddar cheese sauce are an adequate substitute for Velveeta.

WISCONSIN BEER CHEESE CHOWDER

5 cups broccoli florets

2 cups chopped carrots

½ cup chopped onions

3 cups chicken broth

¾ cup butter

¾ cup flour

1 teaspoon dry mustard

2 teaspoons white pepper

5 cups milk

1 (8-ounce) package softened cream cheese

2 pounds Velveeta, cubed

1 pound cooked Polish sausage, cubed

1 cup flat beer

Combine broccoli, carrots, onions, and chicken broth in a medium saucepan. Bring to a boil, reduce heat, cover, and simmer 10 to 15 minutes or until tender. Remove from heat. Set aside and do not drain.

Melt butter in a large kettle. Stir in flour, dry mustard, and pepper. Add milk all at once. Cook and stir until thick, about 10 minutes.

Place cream cheese in a mixing bowl. Stir in 1 cup of the hot milk mixture. Beat until smooth and creamy. Pour back into kettle. Add cheese, sausage, beer, and undrained vegetables. Heat through at low temperature.

MAKES 1 GALLON

Lake Michigan and the bay of Green Bay flank the seventy-mile-long peninsula that is Door County. Along three hundred miles of shoreline are eleven historic lighthouses and an extensive maritime heritage. About two million people visit per year, but year-round population hovers at twenty-eight thousand.

Within the county are 5 state parks, 19 county parks, 180 holes of golf, and at least 50 public beaches. No location in Wisconsin grows more cherries; the tart Montmorency is the most common, and it shows up in all courses at restaurants, especially during mid-summer harvesting. doorcounty.com, (800) 527-3529

Plantation Supper Club

11084 Highway 70, Woodruff
(715) 356-9000
plantationsupperclub.com
Owners: Tom and Lynn Gumhold

Resilience is the ability to recover from life's difficulties, and that type of toughness is an underlying theme at the Plantation.

When the business opened on July 1, 1938, it was serving fried chicken and had a wall of slot machines in the dining room, craps tables elsewhere, and a wire hookup to receive horse race and baseball game results. Acrobats, tap dancers, musicians, and singers took the stage to entertain.

The Reno-esque casino was off to a fast start and abrupt intrusion. Gunmen killed a security guard and broke into the house within four days. Gone were eight slot machines and profits from Fourth of July gambling. It was enough to close the Plantation for a year and subdue it. Instead of boasting an abundance of games of chance, the reopened supper club called itself a "meeting place for you and your friends," even though gambling and floor shows continued. The business only operated during the peak of summer, July through August, until the 1950s.

Wally and Verla Gumhold got to know the Plantation while taking vacations from their Milwaukee restaurant, but that world was jolted in 1968 by the war in Vietnam. The Army took two Gumhold sons, Richard and Tom, overseas but in different directions. Tom, a foot soldier, returned. His older brother, a tank operator, was electrocuted. Within a year their grief-stricken parents sold their restaurant and retired to a Northwoods cottage, but Wally wasn't idle for long.

The Plantation
ARBOR VITAE, WISCONSIN
Cor. Highways 51 and 70 - One mile north of Woodruff

"The Finest Cocktail Lounge in the North Woods"

When a For Sale sign went up at the Plantation, the father gave a call to Tom, who was working for Milwaukee's Harley-Davidson Motor Co. They took a look, were running the place by 1970, and made steady progress until an attic fire caused two hundred thousand dollars in damage in 1974. Tom and wife Lynn, living in an attached apartment, lost all they owned. But before 1975 ended, the supper club was rebuilt and capacity expanded from 120 to 150 seats.

The Plantation sits near the busy intersection of Highways 51 and 70, a short walk from Little Muskie Lake and two miles north of Woodruff, population 966. Wally kept a hand in the business until 1994, two years before his death. Now Tom cooks and Lynn takes charge of the dining room.

Only shelves of supplies separate Tom's little office from his kitchen. He doesn't allow room for much more than a small desk, filing cabinet, couple of chairs, guitar, and music stand where sheet notes for the tune "Walk Right In" are propped. On the wall is a photo of Willie Nelson. The modest setup makes a song within easy reach if it's a slow night in the dining room. "I started playing guitar when I was fourteen and quit for about fifteen years, then started up again," Tom says. "I get a sense of accomplishment from playing."

He says not much has changed with the supper club's menu: Prime rib, served every night, is a draw. So are his barbecued ribs. "They bake long, so they're tender —and that's about all I want to tell you about that," he says, only half-joking. He doesn't use a smoker. On the bar menu are at least one dozen ice-cream drinks; ask for a root beer float here, and you'll get ice cream with root beer schnapps and crème de cacao.

"It's not so much how good the food is, but who you are with" that makes supper club dining special, he offers. The Plantation closes for a couple of months, after Valentine's Day, so the owners can explore other parts of the world. Travels have taken them to Costa Rica, Belize, and, yes, back to Vietnam because of the beauty of the country. Tom shot video of his return trip, made a documentary called *Vietnam Revisited*, and sold it to veterans and the Vietnamese.

Although operation of the Plantation is a key part of Tom's life, the work is demanding and the supper club has been for sale for years. "We had it listed for $1.3 million, and now we are at $850,000, with no takers yet," he reveals.

Milk in 1987 was designated the official state beverage of Wisconsin, and Bos Taurus—the dairy cow—since 1971 is the official domestic animal.

The Badger State also acknowledges the sugar maple as the state tree (since 1949), white-tailed deer as the state wildlife animal (1957), honeybee as the state insect (1977), corn as the state grain (1989), polka as the state dance (1993), cranberry as the state fruit (2004), and Danish kringle as the state pastry (2013).

Although the muskellunge ("muskie") became the state fish through legislative action in 1955, you won't find it on restaurant menus. That's because the feisty fighter is more of a prized trophy fish, heavy, bony, and hard to catch: The world record is sixty-nine pounds, eleven ounces, set in 1949 by Louis Spray on the Chippewa Flowage.

Minimum length for a legal catch is forty inches on most of Wisconsin's waterways, and the limit is one. The muskie is the biggest member of the pike family.

*Everybody who eats dinner at the Plantation gets one Cheesy along with a chicken wi__
and butter. The recipe for this two-bite nibble was inspired by a family friend in the L__
area, about fifty miles northeast.*

CHEESYS

Preheat oven to 375°F. Chop the onion and mix it with the mayonnaise. Spoon a dollop of the mixture onto bread slices and top with swiss cheese. Press down on the cheese so the mixture underneath spreads.

Bake 7 to 10 minutes, or until cheese melts. Serve warm.

MAKES 12

1 small onion
1 cup mayonnaise
12 slices snack or cocktail rye bread
Swiss cheese slices
Pepper, optional

smokey's

6410 Highway W, Manitowish Waters
(715) 543-2220
smokeysdining.com
Owner: Liz Uihlein

For at least fifty years, until 2004, what visitors found between Papoose Creek Pines and Toy Lake Swamp was the Oasis, a mom-and-pop tavern that sold food. It was a logical stop for Vilas County hunters and fishermen on the 4,200-acre Manitowish Waters Chain of Lakes.

The location is quiet, just north of 650-acre Rest Lake and almost two miles from the closest town. In the neighborhood are dense patches of red and white pine trees, some one century old. When owners of the Oasis retired, the log cabin with a gas pump and outdoor beer signs sat vacant for a couple of years, until a new owner and her managers came up with a new vision for the property. They bet on a more upscale approach, to suit a higher-end clientele.

After rebuilding, updating, and renaming, Smokey's opened as a sixty-seat supper club that loves meat, potatoes, and more. Order the Tenderloin Oscar or Salmon Oscar, and the fillet arrives with large sautéed scallops, shrimp, crab cakes, asparagus, and a hollandaise or béarnaise sauce. This house specialty is one example of going above and beyond customer expectations for Northwoods dining.

"Our draw is the food—we don't want to be known as a bar," says General Manager Jim Zett. "People don't come here to get slobbering drunk." He

describes himself and wife Kellie Zett as hands-on managers who make it their business to know the names and preferences of customers. Their employees are treated like family but held to a high standard: A drug test and background checks are required of new hires. Jim says they also are paid more than the industry average.

All this means that bartenders are social, repeat diners sometimes ask for their favorite server, and info on comment cards is logged. When the dining room's noise level was identified as an issue, a six-figure investment improved acoustics. Chefs stay on top of their game by tweaking longtime favorites and introducing new recipes. "Some restaurants haven't changed their menu for twenty-five years," Jim observes. "If you want a business to grow, you have to be willing to make changes."

He knows his customers tend to eat out more than once a week, so they also patronize competitors, "but we'll continue to do OK if we don't lower our standards or quality." He welcomes groups of sportsmen dressed casually as well as couples "dressed to the nines," with furs, for holidays, or other special occasions.

Being in the middle of the sometimes-wily Northwoods, year-round, suits him fine. The military kid who was born in Germany has lived many places, including Alaska. "I made my life start there," Jim says. "I liked the remote location, the fishing, and the hunting." He stayed thirteen years, employers included Holland America, and that is how Jim learned about hospitality. When his parents retired to Northwoods Wisconsin, he came to visit and ended up staying, cooking for another supper club, marrying, becoming a father, and fostering an appreciation for the four distinct seasons that Manitowish Waters experiences every year.

The Joy of Cooking *traces schaum torte recipes to the 1870s and German immigrants in Wisconsin. The dessert originally called for a whipped cream filling; ice cream showed up as a substitute by the 1950s and remains a customary part of the presentation. The German translation for the treat is "foam cake."*

At the base of schaum torte is a dried and airy meringue shell. It is filled with ice cream and usually topped with strawberries, but Smokey's Chef Pat Sheeley prefers a finishing touch of raspberry puree. Using fresh fruit for the puree is fine, but he considers that a waste of fresh berries when a bag of frozen ones works just as well. So restrain yourself and simply use a fresh raspberry or two to garnish this long-loved supper club classic.

SCHAUM TORTE

For the base:

½ cup egg whites (from 4–6 eggs)

1 teaspoon vinegar

1 tablespoon vanilla

1 cup sugar

For the filling:

1 (16-ounce bag) frozen raspberries

1 cup sugar, or to taste

2 cups vanilla ice cream

Preheat oven to 275°F. Beat egg whites until just foamy, about 2 minutes. Add vinegar and vanilla; beat until soft peaks form. Add 1 cup sugar, ¼ cup at a time, and wait 30 seconds between these additions. Beat until stiff peaks form.

Put parchment paper on a cookie sheet and lightly cover with cooking spray. Fill pastry pipe with beaten egg whites and pipe out 4- to 5-inch disks. Then pipe a wall around the outer edge of each disk. (If not using a pastry pipe, spoon out 4-inch mounds of the beaten egg whites and make an indentation in the middle of each mound.)

Place cookie sheet in oven. After 1 hour, turn off temperature. Crack open the oven door and remove the cookie sheet 1 hour later.

Combine raspberries and 1 cup sugar in a saucepan. Add water, just to cover. Bring to a boil over medium-high heat. Lower heat and simmer 1 hour, or until mixture thickens, stirring occasionally. When sauce cools, pour raspberry mixture into a food processor or immersion blender. Blend until consistency is smooth. Press the mixture through a fine mesh strainer to remove seeds. Return to the stove for additional thickening, if necessary; sauce will stick to the back of a spoon when done.

To serve, place a scoop of ice cream on each meringue shell and top with raspberry sauce.

SERVES 4

TALLY HO SUPPER CLUB

10432 Highway 77, Hayward
(715) 462-3646
tallyhosupperclub.com
Owners: Steve and Lorrie Conlon

A stone fireplace and windows on the Tally Ho's north wall are all that remain of the original restaurant that opened in 1946, after Civilian Conservation Corps barracks were hoisted onto runners in winter and pulled along icy roads to the outskirts of Chequamegon–Nicolet National Forest, fifteen miles east of Hayward.

Owners Clyde and Esther Magill set up a meeting place for friends and respite for travelers that supplied home cooking and libations (an old-fashioned cocktail cost sixty-five cents back then). Ice chiseled from a nearby lake and packed in sawdust would preserve provisions—meats, vegetables—during the heat of summer.

It wasn't until 1967 that the supper club got a makeover to the English Tudor motif that diners experience today. Subsequent owners added a dance floor and piano lounge and expanded the barroom. Much of the cozy, lodge-inspired

decir is a nod to the popularity of hunting, especially for deer in autumn, and Executive Chef Susan Birkey pays attention to this on her menus.

"Nearly everyone in this area hunts," she says, and that makes game an attractive meal option and topic for her occasional cooking demos in the Hayward area. Her slow roasting of whole ducks takes an entire afternoon; accompanying the birds is a complex sauce that blends plum wine with ginger, star anise, and other flavors.

Susan also is a certified dietary manager, which means she knowledgeably addresses special dietary needs, especially when customers call to mention this before dining at the Tally Ho. She thinks more chefs should have this credential because "the number of clients requiring special dietary consideration is definitely on the upswing."

When Susan talks about a return of the relish tray to her supper club, it's not as simple as matching raw veggies with a commercial dip; this chef prefers visions of Italian crostini and a green/black olive tapenade.

The Minnesota farm girl was introduced to the Hayward area as a child, while vacationing with family. She was hired as sous chef at the Tally Ho in the 1990s, then returned to her home state for restaurant work. A traveling fish purveyor made her aware of Tally Ho's need for an executive chef; he also observed that Susan and the supper club's owner, Chuck Massaro, were his only customers who sought cold water lobster tails. "They are more expensive," Susan explains, "but better in flavor and texture."

She was back at the Tally Ho around 2010, bringing with her a recipe for pork prime rib with mushroom Marsala sauce. This is a well-received twist to traditional supper club meats, as are her lemon pepper pork chops, which go beyond a few shakes of commercial lemon pepper seasoning. Her version is a from-scratch sauce that uses Meyer lemons. "I don't have a shortage of ideas," she says.

Since 1990, ownership of the Tally Ho has changed five times. Former owners Chuck and JoKaren Massaro have re-engaged with the business. The cooking crew includes Taylor Mills, Susan's husband. The supper club is closed from mid-October to early December, when it reopens for holiday parties. Winter business hours are abbreviated.

Susan Birkey prefers using organic ingredients and duck from Indiana-based Maple Leaf Farms for this pan-seared starter course, which is an occasional special at the Tally Ho.

PAN-SEARED DUCK BREAST APPETIZER

Combine vinaigrette ingredients. Set aside.

Preheat oven to 375°F. Use sharp knife to score the duck breasts, skin side up. Season with kosher salt and pepper.

Pour oil into preheated, ovenproof skillet. Use tongs to gently add duck breasts, skin side down. Sear 5 minutes, or until skin is browned and crispy.

Place skillet in oven for 5 minutes. Remove skillet and let duck breasts rest for 5 minutes while setting up plates. Line each salad plate with a handful of salad greens. Top with sliced duck, fanned out. Garnish with cherries, raspberries, and mint. Drizzle with ¼ cup vinaigrette. Dust plate edges with parsley.

SERVES 4

For the vinaigrette:
2 tablespoons sun-dried sour
   cherries
1 tablespoon minced shallots
3 tablespoons red wine vinegar
½ cup toasted sesame oil
Pinch of salt
Grind of pepper

For the duck:
4 (6-ounce) boneless duck
   breasts
Kosher salt, to taste
Freshly ground pepper, to taste
2 tablespoons toasted
   sesame oil

For the garnish:
Salad greens
Sour cherries
Fresh raspberries
Fresh mint
Finely chopped parsley

The chef celebrates the arrival of cooler weather in autumn with this salad of root vegetables. She developed it after a customer told her, "I'm coming back in late August and love beets." Roast the beets the day before assembling this dish, Susan suggests.

ROASTED RED AND GOLDEN BEET, GOAT CHEESE, AND ARUGULA SALAD

2 golden beets
2 red beets
4 cups arugula
12 ounces goat cheese, sliced
1 cup balsamic vinaigrette
Chopped fresh parsley, to
   garnish

Preheat oven to 325°F. Wash and scrub beets, trim roots, and poke each beet several times with fork tines or a small knife.

Wrap each beet in its own piece of aluminum foil. Set wrapped beets on a cookie sheet and bake 90 minutes. Before removing from oven, stab with a fork or knife, to ensure tenderness.

Let beets cool 15 minutes before removing foil. Use paring knife to scrape off skin, and bumps from beets. Place in a stain-proof container, cover, and refrigerate. Slice beets when ready to use.

To assemble, place arugula on salad plates. Arrange beets and goat cheese on top. Drizzle with ¼ cup vinaigrette per serving. Garnish with chopped parsley or other fresh herbs.

SERVES 4

TURK'S INN

Hayward
Closed since February 2013
Owner: Beatrice "Marge" Gogian

Marge Gogian's life was all about style. She was a New York City fashion designer for decades, until her father had a heart attack in the 1970s and she moved home to help run the family's restaurant near the Namekagon River, four miles northeast of Hayward.

This was no casual, log cabin setting, and it was remarkably out of place for Northwoods Wisconsin. Marge's parents were Armenian, but born in Turkey, and their arranged marriage lasted fifty-three years. Turk's Inn lasted almost eighty, until Marge's death in 2013 at age eighty-five. Almost until the end, she was at the job, even after heart attacks. That includes filling in for waitresses who didn't make it to work.

The restaurant was as much of a piece of art as Marge's world of fabrics and runway models. Most ceilings and walls were hues of red. Linen napkins were light pink. Chair backs were nearly lime green. Holiday tree lights twinkled all year, on archways and pillars.

The menu was exotic for its time and location—appetizers of flaky, cheese-filled börek; kebabs of lamb, served with nutty pilaf; slices of baklava, served with thick Turkish coffee for dessert.

With the passage of time, the restaurant's Persian textiles, Byzantine art, and souvenirs from worldwide travels became dusty artifacts. The once-common celebrity sightings—substantiated by many framed autographed photos—turned into faded snapshots of the supper club's prime.

Patronage at Turk's Inn crossed the political spectrum: Supreme Court Justice Harry Blackmun to the Kennedys—John, Robert, and Ted. How some of them found their way to Hayward remains a mystery.

Wisconsin is home to at least twelve thousand places to eat and drink, and most of the businesses that are independently owned fail within the first year. Turk's Inn did more than just survive. It made its mark as a flamboyant attraction.

The menu stated that "the art of cooking is an art to be proud of" and "eating should be an unhurried pleasure." A meal at Turk's Inn could last three delicious hours, sometimes with the gracious Marge doing it all: taking orders, pouring wine, and serving food from a cart wheeled carefully from kitchen to table.

For all diners in those later years knew, Marge was also preparing the food. And if you did a casual survey, chances are good that most customers were celebrating—an anniversary, a birthday, a reunion, a soldier's return from war—special occasions that deserved a special setting.

Fans of Turk's Inn could call it an at-risk tourist gem and not be wrong. But you also could argue that keeping it open after Marge's passing wouldn't be right. "It was such a legend in its day," acknowledges Tom Shuman, a longtime family friend and executor of Marge's estate.

The dairy farmer, who raises grass-fed beef, knows the property was in need of a facelift because of peeling paint outdoors, duct-taped furniture, and other, growing cosmetic wear and tear. It was hard for Marge to watch, too, but harder for her to fix. "Her mind was so sharp and her memory was so great," Tom says, of his childhood friend. "She didn't like change and wanted things to stay the way they were" during the pinnacle of Turk's Inn.

The supper club, its contents, and its land were auctioned a few months after Marge's death, and that was her adamant final wish. She had told Tom about an Italian restaurant that she loved while living in New York, but when revisiting years later, neither the food nor decor looked the same.

"Something was wrong," Marge had explained. "The parents had left and someone else was in charge. That's never going to happen here." Auction proceeds raised more than one million dollars for scholarships for graduating seniors at Hayward and Drummond high schools. "It's not just for those going to college, but technical schools too," Tom says, especially those pursuing the culinary arts. Just as Marge wanted.

These recipes, served together at Turk's Inn, are a nod to Marge Gogian's Armenian heritage. Back in the day, the spicing was exotic fare, and the pilaf would be shipped in from California, also unusual for the times.

SHISH KEBAB

For the meat:

3 pounds lamb shoulder or beef
    tenderloin
1 teaspoon basil
1 teaspoon cumin
1 teaspoon garlic powder
1 teaspoon oregano
1 teaspoon rosemary
1 teaspoon tarragon
1 teaspoon thyme
½ cup chopped onion
Splash of fresh lemon juice
Dry sherry, as needed

For the kebabs:

4 tomatoes
2 large onions
2 green peppers
1 cubed zucchini (optional)
¼ cup melted butter
2 drops olive oil
Salt, to taste
Pepper, to taste

Cut meat into 1-inch cubes and place in a glass bowl.

Combine basil, cumin, garlic powder, oregano, rosemary, tarragon, and thyme. Cover all sides of meat with this mixture. Add onion, lemon juice, and enough sherry to cover the meat. Marinate overnight.

Cut tomatoes in half. Cut onions into quarters and take apart a few onion layers. Remove seeds and membrane from green peppers before cutting into quarters.

Heat grill or oven broiler. Remove meat from marinade. Thread skewers with pieces of meat and vegetables (including zucchini, if used). The tomato goes near the tip of the skewer, to lessen overcooking.

Combine butter and olive oil; use this to baste the kebabs. Season with salt and pepper.

Place kebobs on grill or broiler. Turn occasionally. Cooking time depends on level of heat and desired degree of doneness. Serve with pilaf.

SERVES 6–8

PILAF

Break up chow mein noodles. Combine with remaining required ingredients in a saucepan. Do not stir while cooking over medium heat until liquid is absorbed, about 15–20 minutes. Remove from heat. Use spoon to flip over ingredients. Let rest 5–10 minutes.

If adding optional ingredient(s), fold in just before serving.

SERVES 6–8

1 cup thin chow mein noodles
2 cups long-grain rice or cracked wheat
4–8 tablespoons butter
4 cups chicken broth
1 teaspoon salt
Pepper, to taste
½ cup butter-sautéed onions, chickpeas, tomatoes, and/or green pepper (optional)

The Village Inn

22270 Highway C, Cornucopia
(715) 742-3941
villageinncornucopia.com
Owners: Wade and Cheryl O'Bryon

Whitefish shows up in almost all courses at The Village Inn because the fish comes from Halvorson Fisheries, in business since the 1970s and less than two miles away. Whitefish are caught daily along nearby Siskiwit and Bark Bays, which feed into Lake Superior.

A delicacy here is seasoned and pan-fried whitefish livers, served with sautéed onions and green peppers. Sandwiches are made with whitefish spread. Whitefish sliders—small, fried fillets—are paired with house-made tarter sauce and chips. As a dinner the fish gets a light cornmeal breading before frying, but broiling is another option.

Fresh trout from Halvorson Fisheries is also a local specialty. It shows up in Caesar salad and as trout Florentine (wrapped with layers of spinach and artichokes in puff pastry). Trout cakes—fish with diced veggies and herbs—are served with a side of raspberry shallot butter. The fish chowder is a mix of trout and whitefish with potatoes, onions, corn, butter, and cream.

The Village Inn   61

Beef from Siskowit Galloways Farm and canned condiments (kraut, beets with sea salt, ginger carrots) from Spirit Creek Farm are other ways the husband–wife owners support local businesses.

That's not all, of course. Traditional supper club food—prime rib, steaks, ribs, shrimp, chicken—comes with the fixings that you'd expect. Lunch options include burgers prepared eleven ways, such as the German (with kraut and rye) and the Cornucopia (a grilled whitefish patty). Available every day of the year is chocolate pecan torte. Add nearly twenty choices of wine and a range of craft beers.

Separate from the main dining room is a bar with table seating, open for lunch, and a group of retirees plays cribbage there every weekday. "We open at 10, they're here at 9:30 and play until 11 a.m.," says Mike O'Bryon, who bartends and is Cheryl's brother. "Sometimes they stay for a beer afterward." His sister and brother-in-law bought the place in 2006 and added a tiki bar, a tent for outdoor dining, and live music for summer weekends.

On dining room walls are old photos, reproduced from the local historical society archives, and they illustrate a backstory of commercial fishing, lumbering, and brutal manual labor during all seasons. On a lighter note, in the bar are many dollar bills that are signed and tacked to the ceiling. "They're for good luck," Mike explains. "Before opening, we had to drink all the open bottles and replace them with new bottles of liquor."

"Corny," as the locals refer to it, has a population of ninety-eight and is near the top of Wisconsin. It is sometimes overlooked because the more tourist-savvy community of Bayfield is just twenty miles east. On tap at The Village Inn and throughout the community is artesian well water. Some people fill empty milk jugs at a well in the town park. "You won't find chlorinated water until Bayfield," Mike says.

The sea caves of Apostle Islands National Lakeshore are a conglomeration of rippled red sandstone cliffs, arches, tunnels, and channels that exist and change daily because of waves from Lake Superior that thrash, spray, erode, and add sediment. No other freshwater lake in the world takes up more space or holds more water.

In winter, thick icicles enrich the dramatic appeal of sea caves. When weather conditions are right, a slick and often windy one-mile hike to the caves from Meyers Beach (five miles east of Cornucopia) is possible. Sea kayaking is the best method for exploring in summer, but how close paddlers get depends on their skill level and the lake's quick-changing moods. It is not an activity for beginners.

The National Park Service property—an archipelago of twenty-one islands and twelve miles of shoreline—long ago was home to Native Americans, then fur traders, lumberjacks, farmers, and fishermen. Rustic camping is possible on eighteen of the islands. nps.gov/apis, (715) 779-3397

SMOKED TROUT–STUFFED MUSHROOMS

Preheat oven broiler. Remove skin from trout fillet. Blend trout, cream cheese, sour cream, onion, and lemon pepper in food processor until smooth.

Place mushrooms, stem side up, in glass baking dish and fill with spread. Excess spread goes over the top of the mushrooms. Microwave 2 minutes, then broil in oven briefly, until bubbly and slightly browned. Add Parmesan cheese and return to oven until cheese browns. Serve with lemon wedges.

SERVES 6–8

1 (8-ounce) fillet sm
½ cup cream cheese
¼ cup sour cream
2 tablespoons finely chopped onion
1¼ teaspoons lemon pepper
1 (16-ounce) package large mushrooms
¼ cup shredded Parmesan cheese
Lemon wedges, for serving

WHITEFISH ALMONDINE

Preheat oven broiler. Place fillets on cookie sheet, skin side down. Sprinkle with lemon pepper. Broil 5–7 minutes, or until meat is flaky.

Spread hollandaise sauce over fish, sprinkle with almonds. Return to broiler briefly, until almonds are lightly browned. Sprinkle with coconut and return to broiler until lightly browned. Serve with lemon wedges.

SERVES 2

2 (8-ounce) whitefish fillets
1 teaspoon lemon pepper
¾ cup hollandaise sauce
½ cup shaved almonds
½ cup flaked coconut
Lemon wedges, for serving

WHITE STAG INN

7141 Wisconsin 17, Rhinelander
(715) 272-1057
Owners: Brian, Brad, and Anissa Widule

Seeing double is likely at the White Stag Inn, regardless of how many cocktails you sip. Two of the owners, Brad and Brian Widule, are twins. See how long it takes one or the other to mention that Brad is ten minutes older.

"He'd say it was the only ten minutes of peace and quiet he ever had," Brian jokes, and Brad knows his brother's retort is that "perfection takes a little more time." Customers often find one twin cooking and the other mixing drinks at the bar. Sister Anissa works behind the scenes, in charge of the books. Mother Karen is retired, more or less.

Grandfather Louie Widule (the names kind of rhyme) bought the business in 1955, then called Laurel Tap, from two sisters. One of the first things he did was order charcoal broiling equipment and create an open kitchen where customers easily could watch the cook at work. The food theater continues today, and the menu still has no need for a deep fryer.

The family takes pride in doing business pretty much the same way as in the beginning, except for adding more fish choices than the Friday fry. Smoked pork chops, a specialty, come from Edelman Meats in Antigo, sixty miles south,

and they arrive with a side of spicy cherry sauce. The charcoal-kissed steaks are a hit, and the cuts are carved at the White Stag. When you ask for an entree "Dave's way," it gets a healthy dose of garlic, just the way the owners' dad loved it.

Customers have one choice of potato (a baked russet) and one choice of salad (a generous but plain wedge of iceberg lettuce). The only topping is three salad dressings made at the White Stag and delivered in a three-bowl server, to ladle on your own.

These dressings—a clear, sweet/sour French; a sweet/tangy Russian Cream; and a Caesar with lots of garlic—also are sold

by the quart. Russian Cream, the most popular, is made in fifteen-gallon batches. Only the brothers know these top-secret recipes, and they plan to keep it that way. They also won't budge on their formula for shrimp cocktail sauce.

Sister Anissa, Brian insists, stays clueless about these things. "I don't mess with her book work, and she doesn't mess with the kitchen," he says with a grin. Now a fourth generation of Widules also works at the White Stag, and the family remains true to their roots.

Behind the bar and on other walls are deer mounts, stoneware beer steins, and long carved pipes from Germany. Under soft spotlights is a large oil canvas of tigers, a 1902 work of the owners' great-grandmother, who based what she painted on a picture. Outdoors, a life-size bugling elk statue, painted white and topped with real antlers, makes the White Stag easy to spot during day or night.

Unlike most supper clubs, which shorten their hours of business as weather cools, the White Stag closes only on New Year's Day, Easter, Thanksgiving, and Christmas. That, in itself, says a lot for an area known since the 1890s as the town of Sugar Camp, population under two thousand and a reference to the area's longtime maple syrup and sugar production.

The humble Laurel Tap only had room for 25 customers. Now up to 240 eat at once, and the one-night record is 678. In-the-know diners expect a wait to be seated, and in the entryway is this sign for the unacquainted: "If you have reservations, you're in the wrong spot."

Brian Widule says he keeps this ice cream drink recipe in a drawer and pulls it out when *ily friend visits from Montana. "She's about the only one who orders it," he deadpans, but *secret's out. This is brother Brad's version of the ice cream drink, which uses one-half as much*

MISSOULA TUMBLEWEED

Place ice cream in a blender, add the four liquors and blend.

SERVES 1

2 heaping scoops vanilla ice cream
½ ounce Kahlua
½ ounce brandy
½ ounce Frangelico
½ ounce crème de cacao

This 1956 recipe was the work of family patriarch Louie Widule, and it is served routinely with baked potatoes. When a White Stag server tells you it's better than sour cream, believe it. Brad Widule also sees customers add this to salad and spread it on dinner rolls. He prefers to use Lawry's Seasoned Salt when making batches by the bucket.

WHIPPED COTTAGE CHEESE

Mix at high speed until more smooth than chunky.

SERVES 8–12

4 cups cottage cheese
½ cup chopped green onion or
   chives
½ teaspoon seasoned salt

Milwaukee native Lawrence Frank gets credit for establishing the first supper club in the United States, but it was in California, not Wisconsin. He also was the creator of a seasoning blend for meat and salad that became the foundation for Lawry's Foods. It is not unusual for Wisconsin supper club operators to favor Lawry's Seasoned Salt in their cooking today.

The namesake restaurant, Lawry's The Prime Rib, was located in an undeveloped area between Los Angeles and Santa Monica (now known as Beverly Hills). Logs of prime rib were rolled in a six-hundred-pound stainless steel cart from one table to the next, with servers carving meat to order. Also delivered tableside was "spinning salad," lettuce atop crushed ice in a big metal bowl, and the notion of serving this before the entree was a novel idea at the time.

For $1.25, a diner would get the salad, a thick slab of prime rib au jus, a baked potato with butter and chives, and Yorkshire pudding. The Diamond Jim Brady cut of meat was thicker than average, and the English cut was three thin slices of meat.

Although The Prime Rib made several other entree choices available, they were dropped during the first year of business. Other Lawry's restaurants would subsequently open in Chicago, Dallas, Las Vegas, and Asian locations.

Besides the supper club concept, Mr. Frank gets credit for the introduction of doggie bags and valet parking. Lawry's Seasoned Salt, a blend of seventeen herbs and spices, at the beginning was produced by brother Ralph in a small room of a potato chip factory in 1938. By 1950 it was being sold in glass jars. By 1960 at least two thousand restaurants nationwide were buying the product. Today the seasoning is part of McCormick & Company.

Since 1956, Lawry's The Prime Rib has hosted a pregame feast of prime rib for teams competing in the Rose Bowl. The meal is nicknamed the "Beef Bowl," and it is not unusual for each team to consume at least five hundred pounds of meat.

Central Wisconsin

The middle swath of Wisconsin adds crucial credibility to our "America's Dairyland" nickname. More than six hundred kinds of cheese are crafted statewide, much from the milk of ten thousand dairy farms, many of which are located here.

Factor in master cheesemakers, who earn advanced certification through European-inspired training. They help ensure that Wisconsin routinely wins the most awards in national competitions, and some of these cheeses gain international recognition.

Also of note: cranberry production. No state produces more than Wisconsin. Our vegetable harvests rank high nationally, too, and much of the seasonal bounty is capitalized upon by supper club cooks in rural hamlets to larger communities.

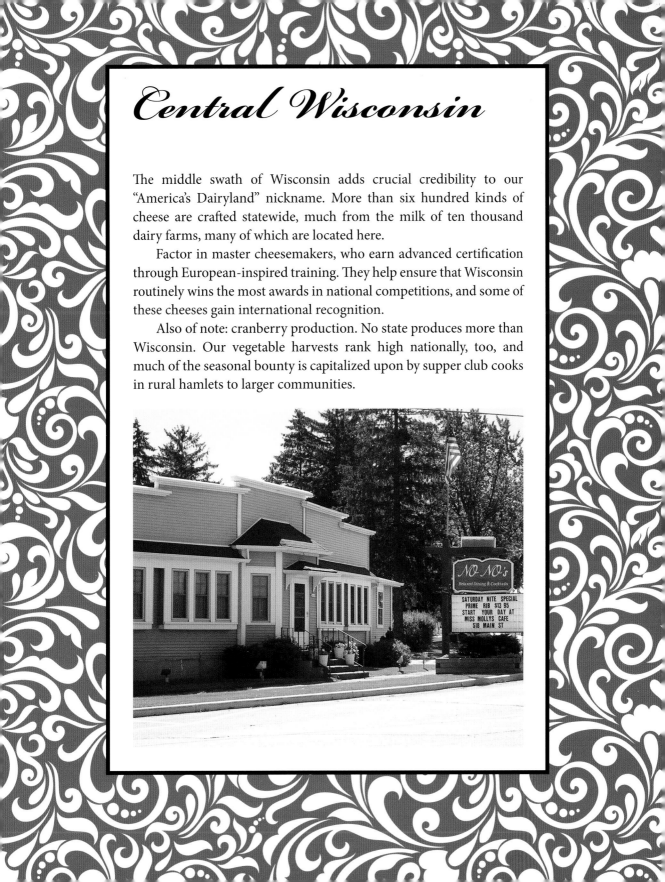

al corso of collins

20931 Main Street, Collins
(920) 772-4056
alcorsorestaurant.com
Owners: Dave and Alex Salm

Seems like almost everybody wants to call al corso a supper club, except for the people who own the business, Dave and Alex Salm. They prefer "fine dining in a casual atmosphere."

Watch them wince when reminded that al corso is listed on a regional supper club map and a statewide supper club website. "That term is so outdated," Dave says. "It's a standard relish tray, steak on a metal plate, and iceberg lettuce. That's not bad, but the eating habits of people have changed dramatically."

But, like the traditional supper club, al corso aims to build a sense of community. Occasional events pair wine or beer with a set menu of multiple courses. The Salms also are establishing a United States Whiskey Society chapter at al corso, and foreign whiskey tastings will be accompanied by three-course meals.

To an urban crowd, dues of $399 to cover five such events per year might seem like a bargain, but this neighborhood's average farmer or laborer won't likely see it that way. "People in our bigger cities—Appleton, Green Bay—will

make the drive to get a dining experience instead of an eating experience," Dave says.

The rerouting of Highway 32, decades ago, almost took unincorporated Collins off of the map. Fewer than two hundred people live here, and dam construction on Mud Creek during the 1960s ensures marshy terrain all year.

Collins used to have two grocery stores, two car dealerships, a barber, a farm feed mill, and more. Little of this remains, so what is left is a relatively nondescript community that almost seems swallowed up by the forty-two-hundred-acre Collins Marsh Wildlife Area.

One exception makes Collins worth the drive, even after the sun sets on the wildlife-rich wetlands, and that is al corso. Customers in comfortable dress feast on Chicken Roulade (the stuffing mixes spinach, gorgonzola, prosciutto); Horseradish Crusted Salmon (topped with a citrus-mustard sauce); Pan-Seared Ahi Tuna with Red Pepper Risotto; Shrimp-Scallop-Lobster Kebabs with Sun-Dried Tomato Cream Sauce; and more.

Add game meats: venison, wild boar, alpaca. The contemporary American menu is unusual for rural Wisconsin, which favors deep-fried fare, but the Salms got rid of their chicken Broaster, and the fries that accompany blackened or traditional burgers are about the only things immersed in hot oil.

Alex and Dave are longtime restaurant workers who became caterers before opening al corso in 2007. He takes charge of the cooking and is a former food service director for a rural Catholic seminary. She heads the business side of operations.

Why land in Collins? Although the price was right for the rundown building that turned into their restaurant, the Salms say they ended up spending about twenty times more than the purchase price to rehab the 1800s structure. The work took about twenty months.

Alex says none of the contractors wanted to put up business signs, for a while, because of the project's precarious nature. All turned out well: A former garage is the restaurant kitchen. The building's original copper ceiling survived, as did a mid-room pole that supports beams and upholds history. While in business as Bud and Tiny's saloon, patrons who climbed the pole and touched the ceiling would earn a drink or candy bar.

Now we have a dinner-only restaurant with forty-six seats and a name that is an Italian reference to being at the main street or center of activity. That's what it was, long before the Salms took ownership. As Bud and Tiny's, deer hunters would head here to register their harvest and tip a cold one. "It was the cornerstone of the community," Alex says.

She considers the restaurant "definitely destination dining," noting the lack of other businesses to bring traffic into town. Word of al corso spread when the Salms printed and gave away three thousand dollars worth of ten-dollar gift certificates, but they have pursued little else in paid advertising.

House-made and long-simmering sauces, soups, salsas, and salad dressings deviate from conventional restaurant fare for the area. Consider the "hint of Guinness" beer that Alex adds to his french onion soup, the Caesar salad whose romaine is grilled, and the Chicken Mulligatawny soup.

Chicken Mulligatawny? Fans of "Seinfeld" might recognize it as the stew-like curry sold by the Soup Nazi. Dave's version, the signature soup at al corso, has a tomato cream base and Cajun flavor. He also bakes his own breads. Gluten-free and vegetarian fare is available, but Alex advises customers to mention these preferences when making a dinner reservation.

For dessert, a specialty is unusual versions of crème brûlée such as malted milk, butterscotch with currants, and bacon-cranberry. Restaurant staffers learn, and learn to appreciate. "It's fun to see their palates evolve," Alex says, be it for fine wine or bacon-wrapped scallops served with an apple dipping sauce.

"People who come here know what they're looking for," she says. Translation: Customers who seek the unexpected will find it.

Experiment with cheese combinations to vary the flavor profile of this potato casserole. Dave Salm prefers smoked cheddar from Vern's Cheese and chèvre from LaClare Farm, two businesses within thirty miles of al corso.

AU GRATIN POTATOES

Preheat oven to 400°F. Coat a 9 x 13 x 2-inch pan with nonstick cooking spray.

In a large bowl, whip eggs with whipping cream. In a second bowl, blend the smoked cheddar, cheddar, and chèvre cheeses. Use a grater or mandoline to slice potatoes ⅛ inch thick.

Spread a little egg-cream mixture into the prepared pan. Add a layer of sliced potatoes. Sprinkle with salt and pepper. Next comes a layer of cheeses. Repeat the layering until all ingredients are used. End with cheeses as the topping.

Cover pan with aluminum foil. Bake 30 minutes at 400°F. Reduce heat to 350°F, remove foil, and bake another 30 minutes, or until potatoes are fork-tender. Cool 5 minutes before serving by the scoop or slice.

SERVES 12

6 eggs
3 cups heavy whipping cream
2½ cups shredded smoked cheddar cheese
1 cup shredded cheddar cheese
1 cup chèvre
4–5 potatoes
Salt, to taste
Pepper, to taste

Wisconsin's least-heralded brewer doesn't make beer. It makes fifty kinds of specialty malts for the food and beverage industry. These worldwide businesses use the malt in malted milk shakes, balls of malted milk candy, beer, bread, cereals, pet food, and more.

Briess Malt & Ingredients Company, in Chilton, says it produces more kinds of malt than any other company in the world and that its products are used by about 80 percent of the nation's commercial brewers. Company founder Ignatius Breiss, a native of Czechoslovakia, made malt for brewers there in 1876. Third-generation malt maker Eric Breiss immigrated to the United States in the 1930s and eventually acquired the Chilton Malting Company, which had begun business in 1901. breiss.com, (920) 849-7711

THE ALTONA SUPPER CLUB

2306 Calumet Drive, New Holstein
(920) 898-5255
altonasupperclub.com
Owners: Dave Braun and Jason Hunsader

The Holyland, about one hundred square miles of east-central Wisconsin farmland and rolling hills, earned its name long ago because scores of Catholic German immigrants settled here during the mid-1800s. Poor crop yields drove them from their homeland of Prussia. By 1870 eleven churches were erected amid the fields of corn and grain; from most of these faith communities sprouted little rural towns such as St. Peter, St. Anna, Jericho, Marytown, and Johnsburg. Still operating in Mount Calvary, population 760 and one of the bigger hamlets, is a seminary high school with two hundred students, founded in 1860.

The other rural church schools are shuttered, and congregations share clergy. Most of the still-open parishes are lovingly maintained and grow more remarkable with the passage of time, because the furnishings, stained glass, and decor are original. This is thanks to the devout churchgoers: It is not unusual

to see a Virgin Mary statue in the yards of average households, but after Mass the most important community gathering space is the supper club. They have loyal, hyper-local followings.

Near the northeast edge of the Holyland is The Altona Supper Club, which opened in 1937 and remains paired in spirit with a western borough of Hamburg, Germany. On a wall in the bar is a large oil painting of bucolic Germany, the decades-old work of a local teenager. Old-timers add photos from their basements and attics, to remind younger generations that Altona used to be more than a place to eat. The farming town by 1901 was swallowed up by the larger city of New Holstein. It didn't help that railroad mail carriers were confusing little Altona with the larger Altoona, in western Wisconsin.

There is little public evidence of the Altona community's existence today. The supper club was built in the country, surrounded by fields of hay and corn. Dave Braun says his business long ago had a separate room to feed thrashing crews (farmers who worked as one team to harvest grain, farm to farm, until everybody's crop was reaped).

Supper club ownership changed hands several times, until Dave's parents (Glenn and Bridget Braun) took over in 2006. By that time it was called Hunter's Rae, and part of the Braun family's work was to restore the original name and building. One year later Dave and longtime employee Jason Hunsader took

over as co-owners. They work hard to keep dinner prices below twenty dollars, and some specials are under ten dollars. Early bird diners (those who arrive before 5 p.m.) sometimes get a two-dollar discount per person, and that might even apply to Altona's popular all-you-can-eat buffets.

"This was your main wedding destination in the 1960s to 1990s," Dave remarks, after a middle-aged couple raved about their daughter's wedding reception and paid the bill for it. They had 120 guests who drank twenty-six pitchers of beer and nine bottles of wine, all a little on the light side. A crowd of 250 to 300 is more typical, as is serving a hearty, family-style meal of chicken and tenderloin tips. "We offer a third meat for the same price" per plate, David says.

Dancing to polkas by the Jerry Schneider and Gene Birschbach bands no longer happens here on Sunday afternoon, but Green Bay Packer parties might help a local family pay medical bills. This happens by charging a flat fee for food and tap beer (or, for children, tap soda) and raffling prizes donated by local businesses. It's the kind of place where a customer who orders a drink might well ask the bartender, "You want something?" instead of leaving a tip. That's the bartender's cue to pour himself a drink that the customer pays for.

Completion of Interstate 43 in the 1970s challenged the supper club's business by rerouting traffic. Closure of Tecumseh Products Company's small engine plant in 2007 put 320 people out of work; as of 2014 the forty-acre manufacturing site remained vacant.

Adding lunch service has helped. So have Lions Club meetings, after-funeral meals, and making it a priority to offer, as Dave puts it, "an outstanding meal at a reasonable price."

The price of this pint-size cocktail stayed the same for the present owners' first seven years of business. In 2014 the cost rose from $4 to $4.50. Served most often on Sunday, after those good Catholics go to church? "Exactly," says Dave Braun, who calls it Altona's Famous Bloody Mary Cocktail.

BLOODY MARY

Mix all ingredients. Add ice and garnishes of your choice. The Altona makes room for a mini veggie bar, spearing a dill pickle, olive, and pickled brussels sprout, green bean, asparagus stalk, and mushroom that is pickled in-house.

(SERVES 1)

10 ounces tomato juice

2 ounces vodka

1 ounce Worcestershire sauce

4 shakes celery salt

Touch of lime juice

Touch of Tabasco

Squeeze of fresh lemon

Touch of horseradish, optional

BAR ROOM DESIGN FOR
WHITEY'S ALTONA
NEW HOLSTEIN WIS.

BY THE
CORRECT EQUIPMENT CORP.
HARTLAND WIS
JULY 1961

Breaking Bread in the Holyland is a forty-two-page booklet that describes the rural area's history and highlights, particularly the Catholic churches and neighborhood supper clubs, which are described as "the ideal place to break bread."

It is not difficult to gain a sense of great congregational pride while driving this area's tidy hills, walking its well-kept church cemeteries, or having the good luck to see the inside of a gorgeous little sanctuary.

Among the most well kept is the Blessed Virgin Mary Catholic Church in tiny Marytown, known locally as St. Mary's. The parish was established in 1849 as a log church, which burned in 1880. A second church also was destroyed by fire, so what has existed since 1917 is a stone church of Romanesque style that sits on a hilltop and can be seen for miles. The interior is lovingly maintained and preserved. It takes more than one day to decorate it for Christmas.

Calumet County also produces a map pinpointing thirty-two businesses that tourism officials consider supper clubs and seventy-one places to find a Friday fish fry. The county boldly bills itself as the Supper Club Capital of the Midwest, rationalizing it this way: "It is unknown why there are so many supper clubs, but one theory is because the region was settled by men and women that worked hard in the farm fields and needed a 'night out' at the end of the week. As more industrialization occurred in the area, people worked in factories and looked forward to socializing with their family, friends and neighbors."

Both the Holyland booklet and supper club map can be downloaded for free at travelcalumet.com.

BUCK-A-NEER SUPPER CLUB

D1891 Highway C, Stratford
(715) 384-2629
facebook.com/pages/Buck-A-Neer-Supper-Club/146170468790682
Owners: Tom and Ann Seubert, Roy and Jean Seubert

On a Sunday morning in unincorporated Stratford, one of the clearest local radio stations plays cheery polka music. It seems fitting when Perry Como croons, "It's a good day from morning 'til night," and a yodeler accompanies strains of "Edelweiss" because optimism and ethnic pride are what you'll find in this part of Wisconsin, in addition to bountiful choices inside the Buck-A-Neer.

The dessert table generates the most chatter from a table of after-church ladies, and it's not hard to eavesdrop on their raves. "The cheesecake . . . so light." "The carrot cake . . . so moist." "The chocolate-drenched chocolate cake . . . so, mmm, divine." Portions are petite (especially by Wisconsin standards), to lessen the guilt of sampling more than one.

Ann Seubert makes the desserts. She is generous in the Sunday smorgasbord selections and in sharing the dessert recipes with anyone who asks. This weekly three-hour buffet turns into an all-day affair on holidays.

Chunks of kielbasa are as likely as lemon-peppered cod and barbecued ribs (Tom Seubert's specialty) in the lineup of nine entrees. This is in addition to the Buck-A-Neer's two salad bars. One holds a heaping bowl of lettuce and the many fixings you'd expect to see. The other stocks house-made specialties: dilled cucumbers, kidney bean salad, liver pâté, ham salad, pickled chicken gizzards, and more.

The good eating happens inside of a brick and wood building that had an odd mix of purpose before Dick and Celine Seubert took ownership in 1973. It was a blacksmith shop in the 1800s (the fireplace was the forge). Then it was a place to gas up the car and hoist a cold beer or two. Before known as the Buck-A-Neer, the building was a restaurant with entertainment called Paris Avenue, complete with dancing girls.

Rozellville, unincorporated, is seven miles southeast of Stratford, whose population nears sixteen hundred. The Seubert family's second generation of supper club owners has a commute that's as short as it gets: Brothers Tom and Roy live with their wives in two apartments above the business.

Building materials are a mix of locally quarried granite and quartz, doors and windows imported from France, and a small back bar from Germany. The Buck-A-Neer name began as a nod to the area's passion for deer hunting in autumn, but then took a twist to play up pirate themes.

Today pro football memorabilia defines decor in the supper club's primary bar, but that is not just because of customers' love for the Green Bay Packers. Rich Seubert, Tom and Ann's son, spent ten seasons with the New York Giants as an offensive guard until 2011. He started as an undrafted player and earned first team All-Pro honors in 2010.

A leg injury ended that career, but not before earning a Super Bowl ring in 2007. That journey involved squeaking past the Packers in overtime for the division title, and you can bet it was a tense day at the Buck-A-Neer bar. In the end Rich got his parents to the Super Bowl as well as himself.

After leaving the Giants, Rich and his family moved to California, where he helps coach high school football. Philanthropic activities include the annual Rich Seubert Celebrity Trap Shoot, to support heart research at the Marshfield Clinic. The event brings former NFL players to central Wisconsin and has raised more than one million dollars since 2008.

Neither Rich nor other Seubert relatives are likely to follow their parents as Buck-A-Neer owners, but when the right successor comes along, Ann says she's willing to help the new owners for a year, to get them up to speed and settled.

Until then, if you need her but don't see her, just tell the bartender. She'll likely appear from the kitchen within a minute or two, after one push of a doorbell that's behind the bar.

Ann shares four of her favorite dessert recipes from the Buck-A-Neer. It is not unusual to find at least ten choices on the Sunday dessert bar.

CARROT CAKE

Preheat oven to 350°F. Mix cake ingredients in order given. Beat for 2 minutes. Pour into a 9 x 13 x 2-inch pan. Bake 30 to 40 minutes. Cool. (For a moister cake, freeze before frosting and serving.)

For the frosting, mix cream cheese, butter, and vanilla. Add powdered sugar and combine until smooth. Frost cake and sprinkle chopped walnuts over frosting.

SERVES 15–24

For the cake:
2 cups sugar
1 cup cooking oil
2 cups flour
3 cups shredded carrots
4 eggs
1 teaspoon salt
1 teaspoon cinnamon
2 teaspoons baking soda
1 cup chopped walnuts

For the frosting:
8 ounces softened cream cheese
8 tablespoons softened butter
1 teaspoon vanilla
1 pound powdered sugar
Chopped walnuts, as needed

One of the clearest radio stations en route to the Buck-A-Neer is WDEZ-FM on FM 101.9, and the Polka Jamboree is what you'll hear when tuning in on a Sunday morning.

Host Jeff Heinz, nicknamed the "Polka King of Central Wisconsin," hosts the six-hour show that features polka music from all over the world. In 2006 he was inducted into the Wisconsin Polka Hall of Fame, which honors people whose promotion, performance, or preservation of the music genre helps keep alive the state's ethnic heritage. wdez.com, (715) 842-1019; wisconsinpolkahalloffame.com

GRASSHOPPER PIE

For the crust:

1¼ cups chocolate cookie crumbs

¼ cup sugar

¼ cup melted butter

For the filling and topping:

1 cup whipping cream

¾ cup hot milk

24 large marshmallows

¼ cup non-alcoholic crème de menthe

6–8 chocolate-mint candies or cookies

Preheat oven to 375°F. Combine crust ingredients. Press into a 9-inch pie pan. Bake 10 minutes. Cool. Place in freezer.

For the filling, whip cream until stiff peaks form. Set aside. Place milk and marshmallows in saucepan and stir over medium heat until marshmallows melt. Cool. Add crème de menthe and mix well. Fold in most of whipped cream (reserve a little for garnish). Pour into chilled crust. Freeze 3 to 4 hours.

Thaw pie slightly and slice. Serve with a dollop of whipped cream and topped with a small candy or cookie.

SERVES 6–8

PEANUT BUTTER PIE

For the crust:

1¼ cups chocolate cookie crumbs

¼ cup sugar

¼ cup melted butter

For the filling and topping:

1 cup whipping cream

8 ounces softened cream cheese

1 cup creamy peanut butter

1 cup sugar

1 tablespoon softened butter

1 teaspoon vanilla

¼ cup chocolate cookie crumbs

6–8 miniature peanut butter cups

Preheat oven to 375°F. Combine crust ingredients. Press into a 9-inch pie pan. Bake 10 minutes. Cool.

For the filling, whip cream until stiff peaks form. Set aside. Beat cream cheese, peanut butter, sugar, butter, and vanilla until smooth. Fold in whipped cream (reserve a little for garnish). Gently spoon filling into crust.

Garnish with cookie crumbs. Refrigerate. Serve with a dollop of whipped cream and topped with a miniature peanut butter cup.

SERVES 6–8

PECAN PIE

Preheat oven to 350°F. In a large bowl combine corn syrup, sugar, eggs, butter, salt, and vanilla. Mix well.

Sprinkle pecan halves into unbaked piecrust. Add filling. Bake 45 to 50 minutes, or until center is set. Cool.

A convection oven, Ann notes, does not work well for this recipe.

SERVES 6–8

1 cup light co
1 cup packed
3 slightly beate
⅓ cup melted b
⅓ teaspoon salt
1 teaspoon vanilla
1 heaping cup pecan halves
9-inch unbaked piecrust

GIB'S ON THE LAKE

N110 Highway 42, Kewaunee
(920) 776-1551
gibsonthelake.com
Owners: Mark and Mary Weston

On the Wisconsin side of Lake Michigan are miles of shoreline that average people can walk, and that's just what Mark Weston would do with his dogs after moving back to help care for his parents. One of the places he'd pass was Gib's, a supper club that had been closed for years. Through the windows are unobstructed views of the lake. Across the road from the parking lot sits farmland.

"I hadn't really been around the area for thirty years," Mark explains, "but I decided this was something I wanted to own." His parents lived a couple of miles away, Gib's was for sale and, to make a long story short, the Westons reopened it in 2011.

What began as a simple bar and grill in the late 1920s was demolished in 1984. The homelike, ranch-style replacement building was a supper club for twelve years and, although called Gib's, nobody named that was ever involved. What the owners—three Rohr sisters—did was combine the first letter of their

married names (Sue Gerdmann, Gail Ihlendfeldt, and Karen Berner). Mark says the women remain loyal customers.

Another family briefly owned the supper club in the 1990s, while the Westons were in Alexandria, Minnesota, operating Weston Station, a restored 1950 railroad dining car. It was fine dining in a resort town and occasionally provided "virtual tours" of other worlds. That means the addition of strands of beads, king cakes, and gumbo during Mardi Gras, Mexican foods for Cinco de Mayo, and German dishes for Oktoberfest.

Schnitzel, rouladen, and more were so well received that the Oktoberfest celebration lasted an entire month, and the same cuisine is a part of how Mark's cooking lures customers to Gib's. The Westons started with specials on German Wednesday, then added German Thursday.

Gib's schnitzel, a pork entree, is always on the menu. No veal? Mark says his wife, who runs the front of the house, is an animal lover who doesn't want it served. The couple began working together in the mid-1990s and married in 1999.

Mark describes himself as a self-taught cook who learned from his parents, apprenticeships, and reading. Much of what makes the cut at Gib's is what was successful for the Westons when in north-central Minnesota: steaks, chops, seafood, and pasta. Broasted chicken and prime rib were added because of customer expectations. Dining capacity hovers around one hundred, and almost all of those seats have an easy view of the water. That's also true at the bar. "I feel blessed to have this view every day," Mark says of his workplace.

German meals arrive with traditional side dishes at Gib's, and that includes Mark's version o[f] potato salad.

GERMAN POTATO SALAD

Peel potatoes and boil until only slightly firm. Cool, then slice.

Chop onion. Cut bacon into small pieces.

Sauté bacon until brown. Add onion and cook over medium heat until transparent. Drain off bacon fat and save.

Add water, vinegar, sugar, pepper, and celery salt to bacon–onion mixture. Stir and bring to a boil.

Mix flour with bacon fat until smooth. Stir this roux into the boiling mixture on the stove.

Slice eggs. Add to bacon mixture. Carefully add sliced potatoes. Serve hot.

SERVES 4–8

1½ pounds (6–8) russet potatoes
½ cup yellow onion
¼ pound bacon
1 cup water
½ cup white vinegar
¼ cup sugar
Pinch of pepper
½ teaspoon celery salt
3 tablespoons flour
2 hard-boiled eggs

Klemme's Wagon Wheel

120 S. Wisconsin Drive, Howards Grove
(920) 565-2325
klemmeswagonwheel.com
Owners: Roger Klemme and Kathy Roehl

Broasted chicken is something the average home cook can't duplicate because the proper equipment is only sold commercially. The cooking process is like a cross between using a pressure cooker and a deep-fat fryer. When done correctly, the finished product is juicy, tender, flavorful, and grease free with a crispy, golden brown skin.

Klemme's sells a lot of it, probably more than the average supper club. In the kitchen of this brother–sister operation are nine Broasters, seven of which are used every week. The first was purchased when the supper club opened in 1972, and the last was added around 1990.

Each piece of the equipment cooks ten half-chickens at once, and it takes only nine and a half minutes. The quantity equals forty pieces or at least one dozen servings of chicken. "It's not that much to me, but maybe to you," Roger Klemme says.

Before the process begins, the chickens are immersed into brine for at least twenty-four hours and then held in a temperature-controlled vat until needed. Roger demonstrates a little ingenuity by using a recycled bulk tank (which is what farmers use to keep fresh milk cool), and that keeps the brined chicken in a safe holding pattern.

As orders come in, the drained poultry is dusted with seasoned flour and spread onto cookie sheets. "It's easy," Roger says, with a shrug. When talking about all this in September, business has slowed to around two hundred pounds of the chicken served per week; although always offered, the chicken is a daily special on Wednesday and Thursday.

The record high for Klemme's is three and a half tons of chicken served in a week, thanks to a huge swoop of weddings and graduation parties. Up to 150 diners are seated at once for these events, and although Klemme's only serves breakfast and lunch to the public on Sunday, owners also book meals for funerals and other special events; food typically is served family style.

"We have lots of repeat customers, and we don't advertise much. It's word of mouth," Roger says. "We support a lot of local groups and the schools. We get their banquet business—the cross-country team was just here. They help you, and you help them, you know?"

When Rey and Bernice Klemme opened their supper club, he was fifty-five years old and the town assessor. His work with Kingsbury Breweries ended because the Sheboygan brewery closed, so this seemed like an opportune time to test his longtime dream of operating a restaurant. Bernice died in 1987, and the kids took over after Rey's passing in 2004.

What the Klemmes bought was a tavern that sold burgers, hosted a Friday fish fry, and was in need of major renovation. Soon the business expanded into a neighboring shop. Roger, age twenty-four when the supper club opened, was working at the Borden cheese plant during those early years. Now he works the bar at Klemme's while wife Pat is "boss of the kitchen" and sister Kathy Roehl manages the front of the house. They stay faithful to a book of recipes that Bernice Klemme compiled. That includes her frozen tortes, barbecue sauce, and German potato salad (served on Friday night).

For some customers Klemme's "is their social gathering for the week," Kathy says. A few visit two or three times every week. "It's been a good life," Roger says. "I've made a lot of friends and met many good people. Otherwise I'd get out of it."

Kathy Roehl says her son refers to this dessert, served at Klemme's since around 2000, as a little of heaven. It is especially popular when strawberries ripen locally, during early summer.

FRESH STRAWBERRY TORTE

Preheat oven to 400°F. Combine crust ingredients and pat lightly onto the bottom of a 9 x 13 x 2-inch pan. Bake 15 minutes. Cool.

Mix filling ingredients in order listed. Spread over cooled crust.

Hull strawberries, set aside 6 to 12 of the berries, and slice the rest.

Combine cornstarch and water in saucepan. Stir until thick, smooth, and brought to a boil. Remove from heat. Stir in flavored gelatin and sugar. Add sliced strawberries. Spread over filling in the pan. Cool.

Add whipped topping, as desired, as the top layer or as a garnish. Slice reserved berries in half and arrange on top of torte, one per serving slice.

SERVES 12–24

For the crust:
½ cup butter
¼ cup brown sugar
1 cup flour
½ cup chopped nuts

For the filling:
8 ounces softened cream cheese
16 ounces whipped topping
¼ cup powdered sugar

For the topping:
2 pints strawberries
5 tablespoons cornstarch
1½ cups cold water
1 (3-ounce) package strawberry-
 flavored gelatin
3 tablespoons sugar
Whipped topping, to garnish

The words *Broaster* and *Broasted* are trademarks of the Broaster Company of Beloit, Wisconsin, which began business in 1954 after founder L. A. M. Phelan invented the cooking process. The company's equipment is only sold commercially, and customers include at least one thousand restaurant operators in Wisconsin. Product lines also include marinades and seasoning blends.

The average home cook's inability to duplicate this food preparation method, which combines pressure cooking and deep-frying, is a part of what makes this type of chicken popular at supper clubs. The Broaster Company says the proprietary process seals in the natural juices of chicken while sealing out almost 100 percent of the cooking oil, resulting in poultry that "has the taste of fried chicken but is moister and less greasy." broaster.com, (608) 365-0193

MAJERLE'S BLACK RIVER GRILL

5033 Evergreen Drive, Sheboygan
(920) 803-5115
blackrivergrill.com
Owners: John and Tracy Majerle

The people of Sheboygan County are proud of their German heritage, and certain pockets are wild about tortes, but the dessert's modern-day versions have more to do with fast preparation and affordable ingredients than Old World traditions, complexities, and baking techniques.

The refrigerated treat begins with a bottom crust of buttery flour and nuts, crushed cookies or pretzels, granola, graham cracker crumbs, or something else. The next layer usually is kind of creamy: pudding, a whipped topping, ice cream, cream cheese, peanut butter, or a blend of ingredients. Coconut, fruit, poppyseed, marshmallows, flavored gelatin, nuts, or chocolate are among the items to sneak into the filling; some are sprinkled, spooned, or spread as a topping.

Karla Utech, the torte maker for Majerle's, has invented at least sixty torte recipes and continues to experiment with unexpected combinations. She learned about tortes from her grandmother and let her imagination run from

there. The average torte portion is big enough to share, as in twelve squares for the average oblong baking pan. Contrary to European definitions, this is not about one dozen or more thin layers.

The home for Karla's sweet creations is south of Sheboygan in the neighborhood of Black River, which is part of the town of Wilson, population thirty-five hundred. The Lake Michigan shoreline community has its own fire department, town board, and team of first responders; a bar; and Majerle's. The restaurant's

present owners took over in 2006, after several others tried to establish other types of businesses, a tavern to fine dining. Daughter Nicole Majerle says her parents' building began as a bar and grocery store in the 1960s or 1970s.

"It's hard to make a go of it, being out this far," she offers. "You have to know to come here. It's not like you see us while driving and decide to stop." No billboards advertise Majerle's, which is three miles east of Interstate 43, but customers certainly do find their way here, especially on weekends, when lengthy waits for a table are typical. Lunch service tends to be quieter. Time a visit right, and you'll see birds at the feeders or deer grazing in this wooded area.

In 2014 Majerle's won eight categories of the hometown daily newspaper's "Best of Sheboygan" awards: fish fry, old-fashioned, prime rib, dinner, atmosphere, service, restaurant for the price, and all-around restaurant. Nicole, the restaurant manager, says her family is proud to offer "a good portion of food for a good price," which matches her frugal clientele's definition of value.

On the menu are a mix of longtime family recipes, such as seasoning blends and soup recipes. Sheboygan food vendors are favored; that includes Meisfeld's Meat Market, especially for bratwurst, and Schwarz Fish Market.

John Majerle was a restaurant cook and metal stamper before buying this business. Wife Tracy was a longtime registered nurse. "We have a big family," their daughter notes. "If you're not working here, you're eating here."

The Majerle family doesn't want you to think that all their specialties are reserved for the final course. This popular salad dressing carries a kick of heat and typically is served with a combination of mixed greens, fresh strawberries, mandarin oranges, red onion, celery, and sugared almonds. Don't think of it as a rigid combination: Dress up your salad with whatever ingredients are in season. Refrigerate whatever dressing is not used.

SWEET AND SOUR BASIL DRESSING

2 cups olive oil
1 cup sugar
1 cup white vinegar
1½ teaspoons salt
¼ cup dried basil
8 dashes of hot sauce

Combine ingredients until well blended. Serve on the side during the salad course.

MAKES 1 QUART

Karla's oldest torte recipe comes from her great-grandmother, who long ago brought [to the] States from her homeland of Holland. This dessert is a family favorite during the C[hristmas?]. Make it one day before serving, the baker advises. A key ingredient, the Holland R[usk, is a] crispy toast cracker. Karla prefers the Reese brand.

HOLLAND RUSK TORTE

Preheat oven to 350°F. Beat the egg yolks until frothy. In a larger bowl, beat the egg whites until stiff peaks form. Blend sugar, crushed Holland Rusk, baking powder, walnuts, and salt.

Fold the beaten yolks into the beaten egg whites. Gently add vanilla. Fold in dry ingredients.

Pour mixture into an ungreased 9 x 13 x 2–inch pan. Bake 30 minutes. Cool.

Whip the cream. Spread over cooled crust.

For the topping, melt the chocolate and remove from stove. Beat egg whites until stiff peaks form. Fold in melted chocolate and powdered sugar. Spread over torte. Refrigerate.

SERVES 12–24

For the crust:

6 egg yolks

6 egg whites

1 cup sugar

1 (4.5-ounce) package crushed Holland Rusks

1 teaspoon baking powder

1 cup chopped walnuts

¼ teaspoon salt

1 teaspoon vanilla

For the topping:

2 cups heavy whipping cream

2 (1-ounce) squares semisweet baking chocolate

3 egg whites

1 cup powdered sugar

The town of Wilson's best-known attraction is Kohler-Andrae State Park and its windswept sand dunes that hover near the shore of Lake Michigan. Also in the one-thousand-acre park are a beach, marshland, and forests of pines and hardwoods.

Native American tribes found their way here. So did Jean Nicolet, Father Jacques Marquette, and fur traders. Now campers and hikers come for a week or a day. Swimming is possible, but the water is often too cold for comfort and no lifeguards are on duty. dnr. wi.gov, (920) 451-4080

Among Karla Utech's newer creations is an adaptation of peanut squares, which are a popular, long-loved, and cakelike treat in Sheboygan bakeries and grocery stores.

PEANUT SQUARE TORTE

For the crust:

2 cups crushed vanilla wafers

1 cup chopped peanuts

½ cup melted butter

For the filling:

8 ounces softened cream cheese

1 cup peanut butter

8 ounces whipped topping

1 cup powdered sugar

For the cake layer:

1 baked 9 x 13 x 2-inch white cake

For the topping:

¼ cup melted butter

1 teaspoon vanilla

8 ounces whipped topping

2 cups powdered sugar

For the garnish:

1½ cups chopped peanuts

Combine crust ingredients and pat into the bottom of a 9 x 13 x 2-inch pan.

Mix filling ingredients, in order listed, until creamy and smooth. Spread over crust.

Move baked cake to freezer for 10 minutes. Loosen cake edges and carefully flip out of the pan, placing the cake on top of the filling.

Combine topping ingredients, in order listed, and spread on top of the cake. Sprinkle with chopped peanuts. Refrigerate until ready to serve.

SERVES 12–24

> **Within one mile of Majerle's Black River Grill is the James Tellen Woodland Sculpture Garden, a home for the many religious, historic, and fantasy figures that a factory worker with little art training made from concrete. The free-admission garden exists because of preservation work by the Kohler Foundation, which has earned global recognition for this type of effort. kohlerfoundation.org, (920) 458-1972**

mark's east side dining and cocktails

1405 E. Wisconsin Avenue, Appleton
(920) 733-3600
markseastside.com
Owner: Mark Dougherty

The week of St. Patrick's Day is a big deal at Mark's East Side. That's when fifteen hundred pounds of corned beef are served; and in the cocktail lounge a clock begins counting down to the next St. Pat's as soon as the present holiday ends. Enthusiasm is high and ongoing because owner Mark Dougherty is one-half Irish (and one-half German).

Bill and Jan Dougherty, Mark's parents, took over the supper club in 1967, almost twenty years after the business opened as the Normandie. The Doughertys renamed it Chef Bill's, and Mark's first job was cleaning the bar on Saturday mornings. He was in the third grade, and before long he was helping grind hamburger because his father was a trained butcher.

By age fifteen and with his father's supervision, Mark was running the broiler, cooking steaks, deciphering food orders, and more. By 1982 he had a college degree with a business major and made a commitment to the family business. "I don't know if this is what I want to do with the rest of my life," he told his dad,

upon graduation, "but I'll give it 110 percent and see what happens." Now Mark is the owner, the supper club seats 150, and he renamed it in 1987.

His parents had a steak and seafood menu that Mark has run with from there. "We don't want to be good—we want to be great," he says, and that means not buying pre-cut steaks. Diners get certified Angus beef because "it adds tenderness and flavor," and "we want at least a twenty-one-day cut date."

Rhoda Steffel, the supper club's manager, started at Mark's as a line cook in the 1990s. She says the breaded-to-order perch is popular. Her boss agrees and recalls "even little bars used to bread it up on Fridays," decades ago. "They used to almost give it away," but now perch commands a high price per pound because the fish is not as plentiful.

Sales of German dishes are about a third of the average night's food sales. That means meals of pork hocks, smoked pork chops, schnitzels, sausages, and slow-roasted meats. On the dessert menu is the playful Banana Schnitzel, delicately breaded and fried banana slices, accompanied by cinnamon ice cream, drizzled with chocolate and caramel sauces, and topped with whipped cream.

"To me, a supper club is a specific form of dining—a place with a nice bar, relaxing atmosphere," Mark says. His mission statement aims to create "be back" customers, which happens by "backing the community that supports you." That means investing in gift certificate donations instead of coupon advertisements.

Mark's East Side Dining and Cocktails   **105**

Soup's On, whose proceeds benefit the American Red Cross, is one of the annual Appleton fund-raisers that involves Mark's East Side, which donates soup for distribution. This recipe is among the supper club's most popular soups.

CREAM OF POTATO BACON SOUP

For the roux:

½ cup butter

½ cup flour

For the soup:

½ pound diced bacon

1 cup diced celery

1 cup diced onions

8 cups diced (½ inch) raw
   potatoes

2 cups water

2 teaspoons garlic powder

1 teaspoon white pepper

1 teaspoon salt

2 tablespoons chicken base

8 cups milk

4 tablespoons roux

Pinch of nutmeg

Melt butter in a saucepan over medium heat. Mix in flour. Cook roux for 3 minutes. Set aside.

In large kettle, brown the bacon until crisp. Don't drain the grease. Add celery, onions, and potatoes. Add water, garlic powder, white pepper, salt, and chicken base. Cook over medium heat until potatoes and vegetables are tender.

Add milk, bring to a boil, and whisk in 4 tablespoons of roux. Add nutmeg, turn heat to low, and simmer. Add more roux, as needed, depending on desired thickness of soup.

MAKES 1 GALLON

Wisconsin law requires restaurants to serve butter tableside, although baking and cooking with margarine is allowed. "The serving of colored oleo margarine at a public eating place as a substitute for table butter is prohibited unless it is ordered by the customer," states Statute 97.18(4), which became law in 1967.

If a mix of individual, prepackaged portions of margarine and butter is served, the majority of packets must be pure butter. Violators are subject to a fine of up to five hundred dollars and up to three months of jail time. A 2011 attempt to repeal the law was not successful.

In 1895, a state law prohibited the manufacture or sale of butter-colored margarine in America's Dairyland. That prompted the smuggling of margarine from neighboring states.

no no's restaurant

3498 Highway 33, West Bend
(262) 675-6960
nonosrestaurant.com
Owners: Norine McGaw and Mathew Hedges

The address is West Bend, but No No's actually operates from downtown Newburg, population 1,250 and harboring a deep love for smelt in spring. This is when the silvery fish that resembles a minnow more than a bluegill becomes the fish of choice, especially during the weeks preceding Easter.

Some of the area's American Legion posts, Kiwanis clubs, and churches fry smelt on Wednesday during Lenten season, but the fish is not bought locally anymore because of a dwindling supply of fish and commercial fishermen. Lake Michigan smelt runs hit their peak in Wisconsin during the mid 1980s, when smelt easily filled the nets of professional and amateur fishermen.

Today's "smelt belt," as Norine McGaw calls it, is pretty narrow.

Ten miles east of Newburg, an annual all-you-can-eat smelt fry began in 1951 at American Legion Post 82 in Port Washington, where one ton of the fried fish is served in two days. A Chicago seafood restaurant for decades has organized an annual bus trip to this smelt fry, where the locals chide visitors who don't eat the fish tails.

Ten miles north of Newburg is Grafton, where Norine used to manage a restaurant. "I tried to offer a smelt fry there, but I couldn't give it away," she says. It's different at No No's, where two tons of smelt typically are lightly breaded and fried by the time Easter arrives.

"We're known for this," Norine explains. "Some people come here two times a week, every week, for smelt," and it's been that way since she moved to Newburg in the 1960s.

Before March ends, the phone calls and questions begin: "You have smelt?" "How much are your smelt?" "Are they the nice littles ones?" It's an all-you-can-eat meal at No No's: A customer begins with a plate of fish served with German potato salad, coleslaw, and rye bread. Then Norine or a waitress walks around with a new platter of fish, clicking the serving tongs while going from table to table and refilling plates.

Staff wear special T-shirts for the season; each year brings a new design and color scheme. The archives include tie-dyed "Smelt Rocks" shirts and a patriotic "Olympic Smelt Team" in red, white, and blue. Still another design uses Green Bay Packer colors.

Norine takes a break from work in January and February but makes sure she returns in time for her restaurant's Tuesday and Wednesday smelt dinners. "A girlfriend and I get in at 4 a.m. and go through those fish, making sure they're thoroughly cleaned. We play gospel music, polkas, and Christmas music, even though it's spring."

Each little fish is breaded by hand, as orders are placed. "If you bread them ahead of time, they glump together," Norine explains. "Some places buy smelt with a thick breading already on them—that's gross."

An occasional customer will go through a whopping ten plates of smelt in one sitting, but the proprietor just shrugs: "If you're worried about how much somebody will eat at an all-you-can-eat, don't do it. The way I see it, there are both heavy and light eaters in this world."

No No's is a mother–son business. Norine bought the place in 1986, before she married, after managing a different restaurant and deciding "if you're going to do everything, you may as well own your own place." She made her mark by changing the property from a bar to a restaurant: "It went from a bar that served food to a restaurant that served cocktails," she says.

You can bet that she knows how to fix the ice machine, bus tables, order inventory, and "if your bartender doesn't show up, you're doing that, too." She and husband Bill live upstairs from No No's, which is handy when stove hood cleaners show up at 4 a.m. to do their job.

She is proud of the longtime success and longevity of employees. Two kids from one family put themselves through college without a student loan or parental help because of working for No No's. The sixteen-year-old newbies are teamed with veteran employees.

"The new kids on the block are something special," Norine says. "They may be a little shaky to start but get in there and learn fast. Usually it's their first real job." Customers do their part by nurturing these employees; "It's like these are their kids, too. We are a big family."

On a holiday, if No No's needs an extra hand, chances are good that one of the regulars knows how to pitch in and is willing to do so. Maybe that means helping with desserts on Thanksgiving. One of her former dishwashers today is a mason who comes back to No No's year after year to help with a fish fry or smelt fry.

Son Matt Hedges is in charge of the cooking but gets a big assist from German-born chef Emil Schneider, in his seventies and formerly at high-end

Milwaukee restaurants. "He was a friend of mine for years," Norine says of Emil, and No No's is doing more German food specials because of his culinary expertise, especially on Sunday night, when pork shanks show up on the menu.

Norine also finds reasons to throw a party. In December it's Customer Appreciation with a complimentary buffet of food and live music. "Heat Wave" is the theme on a Saturday night in January; people show up in shorts, no matter how frigid the temps outside.

"No No" is Norine's nickname, "something I picked up from a friend." The supper club is rarely open past 10 p.m., even on New Year's Eve, and the decor is all about what Norine calls her "total passion"—golf.

Behind the bar is a 1940s set of clubs, a donation from the estate of a long-time customer. Elsewhere are photos of famous golfers, framed sayings about golf, golf artwork, and golf paraphernalia.

The golf belt where No No's is located is far wider and better known than springtime smelting. Within fifty miles are PGA championship sites that include Whistling Straits and Blackwolf Run.

Five miles southeast is The Bog, designed by Arnold Palmer, one of Norine's favorite pro players. To her amazement he stopped in unannounced while the golf course was under construction in the 1990s. "I knew right away who it was—he sat at the bar, ate lunch (the ham sandwich special and a diet pop), and signed a placemat for us. If I wouldn't have been there, no one would have known that it was him."

The old-fashioned is the cocktail of choice at No No's, which is not a supper club surprise, but the garnish of choice is a zesty pickled mushroom, made with a recipe that Matt Hedges created.

COCKTAIL MUSHROOMS

16 ounces medium fresh
  mushrooms
1 cup white vinegar
1¼ cups sugar
1½ tablespoons garlic salt
2 tablespoons Worcestershire
  sauce
4 "good shakes" of Tabasco
  sauce

Blanch mushrooms for 1 minute. Drain well. Place in quart jar or other container with a cover.

Mix vinegar, sugar, garlic salt, and Worcestershire and Tabasco sauces. Bring to a boil. Simmer until sugar dissolves. Pour over mushrooms. Refrigerate for at least one day.

MAKES 1 POUND

How much do Cheeseheads love brandy? More than a third of all brandy made by California-based Korbel is sold in Wisconsin. In 2013 that equaled 149,260 nine-liter cases, and Wisconsin routinely is Korbel's top market for brandy.

"Food and Wine *magazine* listed brandy as one of the new 'geek' ingredients in cocktails for 2013," notes Gary B. Heck, Korbel owner and president. "For Korbel Brandy, celebrating its 125th anniversary in 2014, we find this very amusing."

He notices a comeback of classic cocktails, such as the old-fashioned and brandy alexander, and updated versions. "It's hard to pinpoint the reason why, but TV series set in the 1960s, such as Mad Men, *have certainly brought attention to classic cocktails."* Don Draper's cocktail of choice is the old-fashioned.

Korbel maintains an online library of cocktail recipes, which includes these two favorites in Wisconsin, both of which call for Korbel California Brandy. Angostura is Korbel's preferred brand of bitters, and 7UP is the preferred lemon-lime soda, but Wisconsinites vary the basic recipe in many ways to make it their own. korbelbrandy.com

THE OLD-FASHIONED

Muddle the sugar with the bitters and 1 orange slice in the bottom of an old-fashioned glass. Add brandy, soda, and ice cubes. Stir and garnish with remaining orange slice and cherry.

SERVES 1

1 sugar cube or 1 teaspoon
  sugar or 1 teaspoon simple
  sugar
2 dashes bitters
2 orange slices, divided
1½ ounces brandy
Lemon-lime soda
Maraschino cherry

Note: Supper club operators tend to list the brandy alexander as an ice cream drink, which means using a blender to combine ingredients because a couple of scoops of vanilla ice cream are substituted for the cream.

BRANDY ALEXANDER

Combine all ingredients except nutmeg in a shaker filled with ice. Shake and strain into a chilled cocktail glass. Sprinkle with nutmeg.

SERVES 1

3 ounces brandy
1 ounce dark crème de cacao
2 ounces cream
Pinch of grated nutmeg

NORTON'S OF GREEN LAKE

380 Lawson Drive, Green Lake
(920) 294-6577
nortonsofgreenlake.com
Owners: George and Robyn Mockus

A mere twenty-five feet from the water's edge on the north shore of Green Lake, up to 150 people at a time dine and linger at Norton's, in business since 1948. Founders Harry and Bud Norton loved their setting and all that the lake represents; Bud operated a marina, and the supper club hosted water-ski shows, sailing regattas, ice fishing, and ice boating events.

All dining tables have a waterfront view. Stone fireplaces, tin ceilings, and ornate inlaid wood enrich the interior. Patio seating and a tiki bar add capacity in summer. In the eclectic crowd is a congenial mix of swimsuits and business suits. "There's not a bad view in the house," says George Mockus. "And it's not a bad office window. We like going to work every day."

For most years since 1975, the Mockus family has owned the lovely setting, first Lucille and George Mockus Sr., then sons George and Peter. Condominium development in 2004 shuttered the supper club for a few months, and ownership for seven years after that was outside of the Mockus family, until George and wife Robyn returned to the helm in late 2012.

"We'd come down here as kids, watch the sailboats and walk the pier," George Jr. says. His parents operated a nearby supper club, until they had a chance to buy Norton's. Rene Paul Amadry, a Paris-trained chef, put Norton's

on the map for food quality in the 1940s and 1950s; he worked in Chicago Loop restaurants until getting married in Green Lake in 1936.

Why not change the supper club name to Mockus? "Norton's had a fishing guide service and was a popular family name here. We figured 'let's keep that going,'" George says. Occasional menu additions reflect customer influence: One example is the Simple (Art) Simon sandwich—a chicken breast with melted swiss on a sourdough roll—named after a loyal customer whose children still live on Green Lake. "You listen to your customers," the restaurateur says, "because they're paying your bills."

Customers have included the late Robert Kennedy, because of a campaign stop, and actor Jack Nicholson, who fished here in the 1970s. Pride of ownership and consistency in food quality are priorities for the Mockus family, and Norton's traditionally closes in March for deep cleaning and remodeling. That might mean painting and new carpeting, or revamping the deck and ladies room. "We want to stay ahead of the curve," George explains.

It all puts the supper club eons ahead of the days when an appetizer of marinated herring in wine sauce cost forty cents and a jumbo lobster tail dinner, at six dollars, was the highest-price item on the menu. A 1969 Mother's Day dessert list included cherry tarts with ice cream, butter cake with whipped cream, schaum torte, and a hot mince tart, each for thirty to forty cents.

Executive Chef Bryan Markel is a New York City native who attended Institute of Culinary Education classes right after high school graduation. He moved to the Green Lake area in 2001 and also is a registered nurse who worked in a hospital setting ten years. When off duty he wears a Markesan volunteer fire department jacket; he is a lieutenant and retired medic for the city's ambulance service.

"Once I had a family, I needed more stable work hours, not work that is seven days a week," Bryan says to explain his switch of career. How many children does he have? "Two girls and one more due today," he replied matter-of-factly in November 2014. Today? "It's OK—her contractions are ten minutes apart," he said, regarding wife Sarah. And how can he remain so calm? "I've been doing this for years." The Markels' son, Oliver, weighed in at a robust nine pounds, fourteen ounces.

Supper club hours suit Bryan, a military veteran who compares restaurant work to the armed forces because both require a clear chain of command when operated well. That mindset keeps the staff and kitchen organized. He acknowledges that newly hired executive chefs want to make their mark by turning

menus upside down and that although designing a menu is fun, he refrains from tampering too much. "I have a 'if it's not broke, don't fix it' mentality. I try to not disturb what's working well."

When hired away by Norton's from a fine dining restaurant in 2014, one of the first things Bryan did was analyze meal tickets. He was surprised to see Canadian walleye dinners leading overall sales. Norton's also is known for its fish chowder (on the menu since 1948) and fettuccine Alfredo. Anything unusual about that sauce? "Not that I'd give out" is his reply. That recipe and one hundred others are kept in a recipe binder that goes back to the 1940s.

Little served here is premade. That includes sauces and soups, batter for cheese curds, and wrapped bacon appetizers. Bryan introduces items such as chicken roulade, cedar plank salmon, fried oysters, and an appetizer of mac and cheese on seasonal menus. He moves from kitchen to dining room three or four times a night, to quiz guests about meal quality.

"They do a great business here—an average of three hundred covers on a Saturday night," Bryan says of his employer. "To survive this way in a rural setting shows you have a handle on what you're doing."

These trumped-up chips show up on both bar food and restaurant appetizer menus. They are a long-time staple at Norton's and a good match for cold beer. Smoked bacon from Nueske's, ninety miles north, is the preferred brand of ingredient.

BLUE CHEESE CHIPS

1 Idaho potato
Cooking oil
¼ cup crumbled fried bacon
¼ cup blue cheese dressing
¼ cup blue cheese
1 green onion

Thinly slice potato with grater or mandoline. Deep-fry at 350°F until crisp, 2 to 3 minutes, stirring carefully to separate slices and cook evenly. Cool.

Preheat oven to 350°F. Put chips on ovenproof serving plate. Top with bacon, dressing, and blue cheese. Bake 3 minutes, or until topping is warmed.

Chop onion into small pieces. Sprinkle on top of chips. Serve.

SERVES 2

Green Lake, whose maximum depth is 237 feet, is the deepest lake inside of Wisconsin. On its shores are at least three public beaches and six public parks or scenic lookouts.

Green Lake, the community, has eleven hundred residents and a history as a resort town that dates back to the 1860s. It is home to the state's oldest golf course, Tuscumbia, which turned one hundred years old in 1996. visitgreenlake.com, (920) 294-3231

PRIME STEER SUPPER CLUB

704 Hyland Avenue, Kaukauna
(920) 766-9888
primesteersupperclub.com
Owners: Gary and Lisa Natrop

Supper clubs are a family affair that runs deep and in more than one direction for the Natrops. Don and Vonnie Natrop assumed ownership of the Prime Steer in the mid-1980s. Now son Gary and wife Lisa are in charge. Another son, Dan, and wife Laura operate Haase's Supper Club (one mile from unincorporated Borth); daughter Sandy and son-in-law Jerry Rupp own Wedgewood Supper Club (just off of Main Street in Omro, population thirty-five hundred). Each restaurant is within forty-five miles of the others.

How do they differ? On the Rupps' property are a nine-hole golf course and banquet seating for 125. Haase's is rural and known for "everything big—portions that are amazingly huge," says Lisa: That means forty-ounce cheeseburgers and cuts of prime rib of up to the same weight.

The Prime Steer is the mother ship where the Natrop kids got their work experience and introduction to supper clubs as a possible career. They were raised next door; only a three-foot walkway separates home from work. Long before their father—an architect and plumbing instructor—decided to follow a dream and plunge into a new occupation, the Prime Steer had endured a name change (it was The Hub in the 1950s) and a rerouting of traffic in the 1960s (so the supper club is two miles from busy US Highway 41 instead of alongside it).

The business succeeds, in part, because of the community spirit that the owners cultivate. "Want to do some baking?" asked a November Facebook post. "Prime Steer will be selling precut Xmas sugar cookies this weekend, $13 for three dozen." Customers also buy slow-roasted beef by the pound—"we sell a ton of it" year-round, Lisa says—but until recently it wasn't a regular menu item. "I'm really not sure why," the owner says, but now hot beef is a sandwich option at the dinner-only business.

"We aim to know your name, your drink, and your entree," Lisa says. "We love the regular customers and can't wait to make the new ones regulars." She and Gary find other ways to gain customer loyalty, beyond serving traditional supper club food. That includes sponsoring fund-raisers for clubs, schools, or needy families because "it is the community that keeps small businesses in business." The Natrops also "try to stay in town to do our business," which means most meats, cheeses, and dairy products are bought from vendors within a fifteen-minute drive.

The exterior of Prime Steer, which seats up to 120 diners, is not flashy in design. Inside, look for evidence of Gary's two big hobbies. He races at the local stock car track during summer and is an avid hunter whose collection of conquests, on display in a glass case, includes a moose from Alaska.

This 1960s family recipe remains part of the Prime Steer's twenty-five-item salad bar today.

COPPER CARROT SALAD

Boil carrots until tender. Cool. Chop onion and green pepper (after removing seeds and membrane).

Mix together all ingredients except carrots. Add to carrots and combine. For best taste, refrigerate overnight before serving.

SERVES 8–12

1 pound carrots, sliced
1 medium onion
1 medium green pepper
¼ cup vinegar
½ cup vegetable oil
¾ cup sugar
1 (10¾-ounce) can tomato soup
1 tablespoon Worcestershire sauce
1 tablespoon Tabasco sauce
Salt, to taste
Pepper, to taste

RED MILL SUPPER CLUB

1222 County Road HH, Stevens Point
(715) 341-7714
redmillsupperclub.com
Owners: Donald and Melissa Thompson

The Thompsons knew about the mysterious mischief making before taking over ownership of the Red Mill in 2001 and moving onto the property. They say the building indeed lives up to its spooky reputation: Pots and pans drop off hooks. Lights flicker. Doors open or close. Calculators post odd dates. Airborne coasters nearly bump employees. Children laugh, but none are seen.

"It's nothing scary or frightening," says Don Thompson, but antics do get your attention. Investigators of paranormal activity visited for a couple of overnights and concluded two spirits—one male, one female—still live here. Don calls them jokesters that tend to show themselves when building changes—remodeling, expansions—commence.

"It takes a lot more than that to bother me," he says.

The business opened as the Tip Top bar and grill in 1937, and the name stuck until the 1950s, when owners erected a decorative windmill that no

longer exists. The cozy Red Mill bar is the original Tip Top, and although the building expanded for dining and a stage for entertainment, fine dining didn't begin until carpeting replaced wood flooring in the 1980s.

Both Don and Melissa managed restaurants to help pay for college. Melissa studied accounting; Don focused on animal science and food science. Soon they were moving to Kansas and Minnesota, where Don had executive roles to manage large hog farms. In the back of their mind was the hope of operating a restaurant or bed-and-breakfast. They looked for three years before deciding on the Red Mill. "It was like buying a house," Don says. "The Red Mill felt right. It was comfortable and brought back good memories."

As part of a farm family and one of five kids, Don would eat at the supper club twice a year, after crop planting in the spring and after crop harvesting in the fall. "I didn't know a lot about operating a supper club but was willing to learn," he says. "You have to love the business to make it work. It's not a big money maker, employees can be challenging and the economy has been tight."

The flip side is his estimate that 85 percent of Red Mill customers are people he knows by name. "We see their kids grow up, and they see ours." The dining room accommodates one hundred, plus twenty-two on the outside deck when the weather is warm. Don handles house management and maintenance; much of Melissa's job is behind-the-scenes book work.

"Fish on the Fly"—streamlined take-out orders—is an option for customers who don't want to linger because they are in work clothes or aren't prepared to bring children inside. The growing number of to-go orders for fish dinners needed a solution because they interrupted staff flow on busy nights. Now it's usually three to five minutes from the time an order is placed from a vehicle to curbside pickup.

The busiest months of business are December, January, and February, and for at least seven years the Thompsons have featured winning recipes from a Chef Showdown that encourages culinary creativity from their executive chef, sous chef, and line cook. Each comes up with one appetizer and one entree (with sides) that he or she thinks will sell well. The foods are featured during a ticketed meal for twenty-four diners, who choose winners by rating appearance, aroma, taste, and the compatibility of an entree and sides. Then a dish turns into a monthly special, and the chef who created it gets 10 percent of sales.

"I let them pick whatever they want—we've had buffalo, elk, marlin—but we'll also make adjustments," Don explains. "I'll look at a recipe and decide 'this is how much I'd have to charge,'" and if the cost seems too high for the clientele ("these are steak and potato people, and so I am"), the chef makes adjustments to improve marketability.

Don calls it a learning experience for everybody and an incentive. "It's a lot easier to reward (front of house) staff for good sales, but how do you reward your kitchen for doing a good job?" He counts Potato-Wrapped Haddock with Dill Sauce as an unexpected Chef Showdown success story—"everybody raved about it"—and sometimes winners stay on the menu for several years.

*This favorite from Melissa Thompson's kitchen—"always requested when gathering with f[...]
friends," says Don—is spread onto cocktail rye, pumpernickel, or your favorite cracker. M[...]
fers to use a mayo that has olive oil in it.*

CUCUMBER DILL SPREAD

Peel, seed, and finely chop cucumbers. Set aside.

Beat cream cheese and mayonnaise. Add lemon juice, dill weed, and garlic salt. Mix in cucumbers and chill.

MAKES 3 CUPS

2 cucumbers
8 ounces softened cream cheese
1 cup mayonnaise
1 tablespoon lemon juice
1 teaspoon dried dill weed, or
   to taste
1 teaspoon garlic salt, or to taste

Executive Chef Tyrone Brown came up with this sauce, which is a popular accompaniment to pork, fish, and (especially) chicken entrees. It is likely to show up at the Red Mill as a monthly special. Refrigerate leftover sauce and use it another time.

PESTO SAUCE

For the roux:
¼ cup butter
½ cup flour

For the sauce:
2 garlic cloves
2 cups fresh basil
¼ cup pine nuts
⅔ cup extra virgin olive oil
½ cup shredded Parmesan
  cheese
1 teaspoon ground oregano
Salt, to taste
Pepper, to taste
1 cup white wine
1 cup chicken stock
1 cup heavy whipping cream

Melt butter in saucepan over medium heat. Mix in flour. Cook roux for 3 minutes. Set aside.

Combine garlic, basil, and pine nuts in food processor. Pulse until coarsely chopped. Put processor on low and add olive oil slowly until smooth. Empty into bowl. Add Parmesan, oregano, salt, and pepper. Refrigerate.

Heat wine in small saucepan until reduced to half. Add chicken stock and again reduce to half. Stir in cream and bring to a boil.

Add refrigerated ingredients to saucepan. Simmer for 10 minutes, using a whisk to stir frequently. Add 1½ teaspoons roux (refrigerate the rest), whisk until thick and remove from heat.

Serve immediately over chicken, pork, or fish.

MAKES 1 QUART

Fifty miles east of the Red Mill Supper Club is Arty's Legendary Cocktails, a small company that in 2012 began bottling four-packs of Arty's Old Fashioneds, to save tailgaters, campers, and others the hassle of transporting all of the cocktail's necessary ingredients. "No need to muddle, measure, shake or stir," the company website states. "Simply twist, pour and enjoy."

Founders Timothy Pappin and nephew Ryan Mijal tweaked recipes for two years before coming up with what they thought was the perfect formula. After their successful bottling of the Old Fashioned Brandy Sweet, they introduced four-packs of the Moscow Mule and Old Fashioned Whiskey Sweet and Old Fashioned Whiskey Sour. Work to expand the product line continues in Clintonville, population forty-six hundred. drinkartys.com

This entrée by Seth Kawlewski, a former Red Mill employee, won a Chef Showdown. Don suggests serving the fish on a bed of rice pilaf.

SALMON GREMOLATA

Combine ingredients for coating. Set aside.

Dredge fillets in flour, then dip in egg. Cover with panko coating and pan sear in olive oil over medium-high heat, 3 minutes per side for medium-rare or 4 minutes for medium-well.

For the béarnaise, melt butter over low heat. Whisk in egg yolks, vinegar, wine, and lemon juice. Mix in tarragon, salt, and pepper.

Drizzle sauce over salmon and serve.

SERVES 2

For the coating:
1 cup panko bread crumbs
1½ tablespoons Italian
  seasoning
1 teaspoon black pepper
¾ teaspoon garlic
¼ teaspoon lemon zest

For the fish:
2 (8-ounce) salmon fillets
¼ cup flour
1 beaten egg
2 tablespoons olive oil

For the béarnaise sauce:
¼ cup butter
2 beaten egg yolks
1 tablespoon vinegar
2 tablespoons dry white wine
1½ teaspoons lemon juice
1 teaspoon tarragon
Salt, to taste
Pepper, to taste

RUPP'S DOWNTOWN

925 N. Eighth Street, Sheboygan
(920) 459-8155
www.facebook.com/pages/Rupps-Downtown/159221940803435
foodspot.com
Owners: Richard and Sandra Rupp

From a pool hall and tobacco shop in the early 1900s comes a comfortable and friendly supper club in downtown Sheboygan that quietly upholds traditions and recipes that are decades old. The handcrafted bar is the same that the supper club's first owner, Everett Elam, installed in 1939. His glass-enclosed kitchen design, which lets diners watch chefs at work, was way ahead of its time.

A caviar sandwich cost thirty-five cents in 1943 at Everett's Lodge, the same price as a cold chicken sandwich. The three choices of potato were hashed browns, lyonnaise, and fried, for an extra ten or fifteen cents. The supper club owner was a generous man who, as the story goes, put aside employee Wes Eichhorn's wages while he served in World War II, then offered the surprised soldier two postwar options: Take the money or give it back and become a business partner. Wes chose the latter.

Ownership changed several times before Richard and Sandra Rupp bought the restaurant through foreclosure proceedings in 1979 and expanded into a former flower shop in 1983. "It was in need of a good scrubbing and new equipment," Richard recalls, and upon opening it as Rupp's Everett's Lodge, the business was one of several thriving supper clubs in Sheboygan. As times and tastes changed, most—The Flamingo, The Hoffbrau, Hoffman's, Top of the First—faded from competition.

POTATOES			SALADS	
		Tomatoes		.15
	.15			.15
Hashed Brown		Combination		.15
Lyonnaise	.15	Shrimp		
American Fried	.15	Lobster		.25
	.10	Crab Meat		.40
		Chicken		.50
Club House		Fruit		.50
Baby Club House	.65	**SANDWICHES**		.40
Cold Chicken	.45			.35
Denver	.35	Ham and Egg		
Caviar	.30	Hamburger		.25
Swiss Cheese	.35	Tomato and Lettuce		.20
Brick Cheese	.20	Ham, Tomato and Lettuce		.20
American Cheese	.20	Bacon, Tomato and Lettuce		.30
Fried Egg	.15	Fried Bacon and Egg		.30
Fried Bacon	.15	Baked Ham and Cheese		.25
	.20	Baked Ham		.30
		Boiled Ham		.25
Coffee, per Cup		Fried Ham		.15
		BEVERAGES		.20
Milk	.05	Hot Chocolate		

"I was overwhelmed," Sandra recalls, about the beginning, "but my husband always wanted to own his own restaurant." He had cooked at a local country club and developed a following.

How did that happen? "I was just washing dishes and cutting meat until two guys had a fight on a Friday night," Richard says. "You want to cook?" he was asked. "What do I know about that?" he replied. "We'll teach you," was the reassurance, and the rest is history.

Sandra, the hostess and bookkeeper, juggled restaurant work with motherhood. Their children were ages twelve, ten, and five when the supper club opened, "and here I was, down here all the time." She'd take off on Sunday night; her husband's respite was Tuesday afternoon. "I remember taking all the invoices home and making piles," Sandra says. Now she and Richard delegate much of their work to others.

The Rupps have seen Eighth Street, the city's main thoroughfare downtown, change from a busy shopping destination to a pedestrian mall with no vehicular traffic. Then the street went through a renaissance that brought in more fine dining choices and the restoration of a historic theater for the performing arts (one block from Rupp's).

Richard laments the slow loss of consumer interest in personal service, be it buying meat from neighborhood butcher shops, or seeking gas station attendants to fill car tanks and wash windshields. "Half of the stuff served in restaurants can be bought prepared," he notes. "Some of these great chefs can

work a broiler and make things look fancy, but they can't cook unless it comes out of a can or a box."

He sees a world where "faster" and "cheaper" seem to outweigh the personal touch and independently owned enterprises, but says the supper club life "has treated us all right," perhaps because he knows what can and can't change.

Omit pickled beets from the salad bar—or use whole beets instead of sliced—and you'll hear about it. Richard says the same would happen if the cozy booths were removed. When people return for sentimental reasons—like the anniversary of a first date or wedding proposal—what they seek is the familiar.

One of the world's fastest tracks for car racing is a twenty-minute drive west of Sheboygan. NASCAR drivers, motorcyclists, autocross enthusiasts, and others maneuver the four-mile and fourteen-turn Road America course, near Elkhart Lake, where racing began in the 1950s.

Now at least four hundred events happen per year, and the speed record is 145 miles per hour. The rural and natural setting—640 acres near the hilly Kettle Moraine State Forest—spells great lounging for spectators and challenging conditions for track competitors. Corner five is a popular place to pitch a blanket. roadamerica.com, (800) 365-7223

What customers find on the salad bar at Rupp's are decades-old restaurant recipes that continue to stand the test of time. Some choices used to be part of a relish tray, brought to each table on a lazy Susan. "The coleslaw always was in the middle monkey dish," Sandra Rupp says. There was always a quintet of choices. This recipe is scaled down because one batch at the supper club equals gallons, to meet customer demand.

COLESLAW

1 cup vinegar
1 cup sugar
½ cup vegetable oil
1 teaspoon salt
¼ cup diced onion
½ teaspoon minced fresh garlic
1 medium cabbage
1 cup spinach
¼ medium red pepper

In a large bowl, whisk together vinegar, sugar, oil, and salt.

Mash onion and garlic with the side of chef's knife until they become a paste. Add to the vinegar mix.

Remove outer leaves and core of cabbage. Slice what remains as thinly as possible. Chop spinach leaves, dice the red pepper, and add both to cabbage.

Keep vinegar mixture and cabbage mixture separate. To serve, whisk vinegar mixture, pour over cabbage mixture, and combine well. Do this at least 15 minutes before serving; the crunch of the cabbage will hold for a maximum of 2 hours.

MAKES 1 QUART

Sandra says this recipe works with cooked carrots, too, but be sure to remove the cloves so they don't discolor the vegetable. Rupp's has always begun with canned beets instead of processing the raw vegetable, because it saves a lot of time.

PICKLED BEETS

Bring vinegar and cloves to boil in a medium saucepan. Add sugar and stir until sugar dissolves. Let cool, overnight if possible, so clove flavor fully develops.

Combine beets and onion in nonreactive container. Use strainer to remove cloves from brine. Add brine to beet–onion mixture, combine, and refrigerate 2 days before serving.

MAKES 1 QUART

1½ cups vinegar
½ tablespoon whole cloves
1½ cups sugar
2 tablespoons diced onion
1 (17-ounce) can whole or
   sliced beets, drained

Southern Wisconsin

Milwaukee and Madison—Wisconsin's two largest cities—are Midwest trendsetters for the arts, entertainment, and culture. A mix of respect for tradition and eagerness to experiment shows up in restaurants, too.

Expect an unusual blend of neon-lit supper clubs that are snapshots of history and ambitious chefs who use familiar foods and flavors to create something new. Be it rural oasis or urban respite, these supper clubs might be decades old or emerging players on the dining scene.

These businesses balance an infusion of craft cocktails, hyper-local ingredients, nouvelle cuisine, and sleek settings against long-loved supper club standards. Their often-unique settings become more endearing with the passage of time.

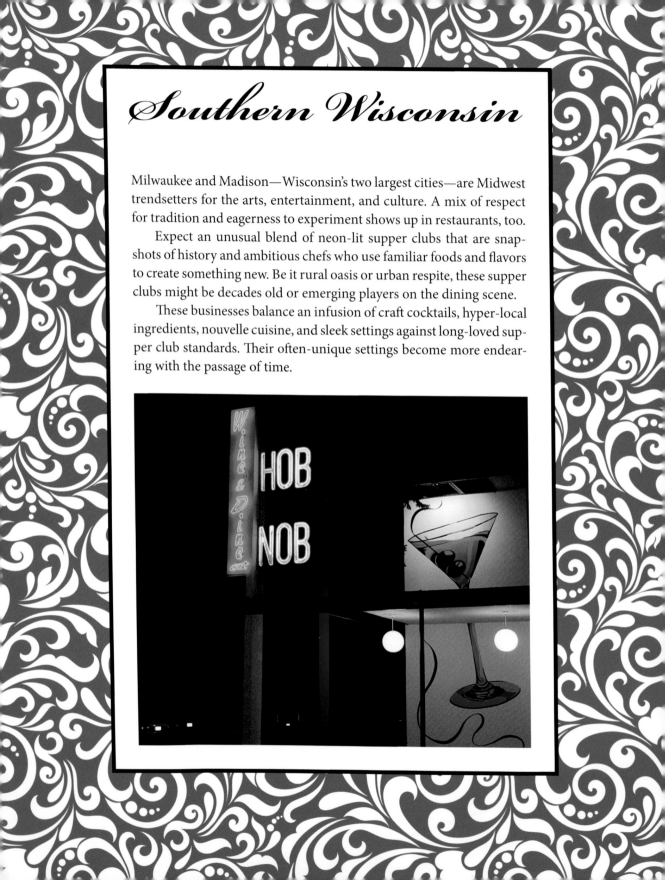

The Avenue Bar

1128 E. Washington Avenue, Madison
(608) 257-6877
foodfightinc.com
Owner: Food Fight Restaurant Group

When a restaurant closes two months for wholesale remodeling, it is unusual for customers to put up much of a fuss unless they fear losing something of personal value. That is what happened at The Avenue Bar in the spring of 2015: Reactions were swift and passionate when the Food Fight restaurant group announced big changes were in the works at the longtime supper club. Consider the chatter of online forums:

> "I don't mind the Avenue changing up its food, but I would hope they would keep their kitschy Wisconsin look. Maybe I'm just sentimental, but that bar room screams 'Wisconsin.'"

> "When I first heard about this, my first emotion was one of frustration. Frustration that no one appreciates what is old, the traditions and patina it takes establishments years, decades to form."

"It will never be the same good old neighborhood bar/restaurant."

Frustrations were fueled by mysteries about The Avenue's future. Would it become a sports bar or trendy dining for a glut of hipsters moving to the neighborhood's new housing units? Food Fight stayed tight-lipped about details, including whether the name would change.

Then auctioneers in three hours sold about everything that defined The Avenue: furniture, dishware, light fixtures, Badger sports memorabilia, beer stein collections, and more. Even the red Badger booth, which sat up to sixteen and was situated below a display case with University of Wisconsin (UW) memorabilia, was relinquished to the highest bidder.

Joey Connaughty, managing partner for Food Fight, says the challenge is upholding traditions while enhancing quality in ways not off-putting to loyal customers. "Look at how this place already has evolved—it changed with the times even back in the 1970s and 1980s," she observes. "I think it is a responsibility of ours to make sure The Avenue survives another forty-five years, to make sure it remains a special place for more generations."

What began in the 1950s as a neighborhood bar with pool tables and orange walls of cement turned into a favorite gathering spot for some of Wisconsin's top movers and shakers. Former owner Skip Zach gets credit for making it that way: Politicians, athletes, and journalists for decades converged here for low-key retirement parties, family celebrations, shoptalk, and reunions.

The business was just a bar until Skip helped introduce a fish boil in 1971, serving it three nights a week. Then came corned beef and cabbage. Before the 1970s ended, dining tables replaced pool tables, and customers expected dinner specials daily. Before the 1980s ended, seating capacity tripled.

When Skip died in 2005, people wondered if The Avenue also would succumb, or change drastically. Relatives approached Food Fight, and the restaurant group bought the business in 2011; for the first four years it remained committed to upholding a few long-standing traditions.

What remained sacred? Prime rib on Saturday, baked chicken on Sunday, and the daily fish fry. Upon reopening in August 2015, only the fish fry remained, and just on Fridays. The recipe continued to use sushi-grade cod, even though it cuts into profit margins and is not customary elsewhere in Wisconsin. Such twists and departures from the predictable are a Food Fight trademark.

"Our restaurants are all 'scratch' kitchens, except for french fries and breads," Joey says. "It's just what we do—we want our chefs to have a hand on everything," in part because "when you make dishes from scratch, everything

has the opportunity to be your signature."

But when a New York strip or tenderloin makes it onto the revamped menu, the meat will be part of a carefully composed dish, not merely a slab of beef with your choice of potato. "This menu has to be approachable from all different angles," Joey says. "A supper club menu offers something for everybody, but that should include adventurous eaters, too." So don't rule out lamb from the offerings.

The Avenue Bar is one of the rare Madison restaurants open on Christmas, which is the busiest day of business, serving one thousand hungry people between 11 a.m. and 8 p.m. The tradition began in the 1970s and will continue.

"A supper club, to me—and don't take it wrong—is an upscale diner," Joey says, because it is a place to feel comfortable, congregate, and interact easily. The evolution brings more seating choices: a meal in the dining room, snacks and cocktails at the bar, or a new fireplace lounge for lingering (a fireplace was removed in 2013 because of disrepair).

"I think people still want the supper club experience," Joey notes, "but they want it stepped up a notch." For some longtime customers, The Avenue's reopening might feel like a divorce, "but we want everybody to feel welcomed, not just the people who have long felt a connection there. We want to bring The Avenue to where we are today and not live in the past."

Bacon sneaks into this side dish, making it a compatible partner for the cheese-topped walle...

BUTTERY SUCCOTASH

Peel and dice steamed potatoes. Set aside.

Melt butter in a large sauté pan. Add onions and garlic. Sauté 4 to 5 minutes, until onions begin to lose color. Add potatoes and continue to sauté 4 to 5 minutes longer, until onions caramelize.

Add lima beans and corn. Cook another 5 minutes. Add bacon. Sprinkle with salt and pepper. Remove from heat. Serve.

SERVES 4

½ pound (3–4) steamed red potatoes
2 teaspoons butter
¼ cup chopped onion
½ tablespoon minced garlic
½ cup cooked lima beans
½ cup cooked sweet corn
¼ cup crumbled cooked bacon
1 teaspoon salt
1 teaspoon pepper

Ordinary cheese-flavored crackers are the secret ingredient for this fish dish that former executive chef Christian Behr would serve with colorful succotash.

CHEDDAR-CRUSTED WALLEYE

Place ground crackers in large bowl. Combine with salt, pepper, and parsley. Split the mixture in half and place into two flat dishes. Pour buttermilk onto a third flat dish.

Preheat oven to 375°F. Arrange dishes this way: cracker mix, buttermilk, cracker mix. Layer each fillet with cracker mixture. Dip into buttermilk. Cover with a final coating of cracker mixture.

Place olive oil and butter in large sauté pan over high heat. Add breaded fillets and cook until golden brown, about 7 minutes. Flip to cook the other side. Remove from heat.

Place fillets onto greased baking sheet. Cover each with ¼ cup of shredded cheddar cheese. Bake 2 minutes, or until cheese is completely melted. Serve with succotash.

SERVES 4

1 cup coarsely ground cheese-flavored crackers
½ tablespoon salt
½ teaspoon white pepper
1 tablespoon dried parsley
2 cups buttermilk
4 (8-ounce) walleye fillets
2 teaspoons olive oil
1 teaspoon butter
1 cup shredded cheddar cheese

This twist on traditional fare, from former executive chef Christian Behr, uses cold-water lobster tail as well as the same sushi-grade Icelandic cod used for The Avenue's fish fry.

LOBSTER AND COD CAKES

4 teaspoons olive oil, divided
½ cup finely diced onion
½ cup finely diced celery
½ cup finely diced red or green
 bell pepper
½ tablespoon minced fresh
 garlic
1 tablespoon lobster base
¼ pound steamed cod
1 pound lobster, steamed or
 butter poached
1 tablespoon fresh lemon juice
⅓ cup mayonnaise
⅛ cup Dijon mustard
2 eggs
½ cup panko bread crumbs,
 divided
¼ teaspoon finely chopped
 chives
Salt to taste
4 lemon wedges

Pour 2 teaspoons olive oil into large sauté plan and place over medium heat. Add onion, celery, bell pepper, garlic, and lobster base. Sauté 5 minutes. Set aside to cool.

Shred steamed cod and lobster in large bowl. Add sautéed onion mixture. Fold in lemon juice, mayonnaise, mustard, eggs, ¼ cup panko, chives, and salt. Mix well. Form four cakes.

Place remaining ¼ cup of panko onto a small plate. Press each cake into panko, covering both sides. Additional panko crumbs may be needed. Use spatula to move cakes from coating plate to saute pan.

Pour 2 teaspoons olive oil into large sauté pan. Place each cake into the pan, over medium heat, and sauté until golden brown and cake is warm in center, about 2 minutes per side. Serve each cake with lemon wedge and ½ cup of Roasted Corn and Red Cabbage Slaw (recipe below).

SERVES 2–4

This versatile slaw was used to accompany The Avenue's Lobster and Cod Cakes and
It is a good burger topping or fried fish side dish. Use canned sweet corn or kernels cut

ROASTED CORN AND RED CABBAGE SLAW

1 head shredded red cabbage

1½ cups sweet corn

½ tablespoon olive oil

½ tablespoon salt

¼ teaspoon white pepper

2 cups mayonnaise

1 tablespoon fresh lemon juice

2 tablespoons Old Bay
  Seasoning

Preheat oven to 350°F. Toss sweet corn with olive oil, salt, and pepper in a large bowl. Spread mixture onto a large baking sheet. Roast 5 to 7 minutes, or until golden brown. Return mixture to bowl and let cool.

Combine mayonnaise, lemon juice, and Old Bay Seasoning in a small bowl. Set aside.

Combine cabbage with corn mixture. Add mayonnaise mixture and combine until well coated. Refrigerate in airtight container.

SERVES 4

Supper Club, an American-style lager, was introduced by Capital Brewery in 2010 as a tribute to Wisconsin's supper club culture. The brewer was named Grand National Champion at the 2013 US Open Beer Championship, and Supper Club is among the labels that have gained awards.

Capital Brewery's work began in 1984 in a former egg factory building, using brew kettles from Germany and winning twenty-five medals for its first brews, a pilsner and a dark, within two years. Now the brewery is a tourist attraction in Middleton, near Madison, and has expanded into nearby Sauk City. capital-brewery.com, (608) 836-7100

BUCKHORN SUPPER CLUB

118802 N. Charley Bluff Road, Milton
(608) 868-2653
thebuckhorn.net
Owners: Chico and Dawn Pope

Retailers tend to make most of their money in a short frame of time—namely Black Friday to Christmas—and Chico Pope can relate to this. His biggest window of opportunity is summer, when campers and boaters on Lake Koshkonong come to call. The Buckhorn is the only supper club accessible by boat on the 10,600-acre lake, and within a ten-mile radius are roughly six thousand campsites.

The supper club doubles its seating capacity during warmer weather, thanks to the addition of a patio in recent years. That means an extra 100 people can dine outside, compared to 110 inside. The Popes also expanded the dock length on the three-acre Buckhorn's three hundred feet of lake frontage.

As the small Buckhorn Bar in the 1930s and 1940s, business was more about quick burgers, beer, and no more than four tables for customers. From a walk-up window, rowboats were rented and night crawlers to root beer floats were sold. Clientele included teams in a nearby park playing kitten ball (a precursor to softball, using no gloves to catch batted soft balls).

The menu gradually grew, and Dawn Pope began making the trek with her parents as a one-year-old in 1953. The family lived on the lakeshore, the Buckhorn's owners had three daughters, and soon Dawn was spending time with them while her parents lingered over cocktails, a fish fry, and dancing on the supper club's wooden floor.

The dance floor disappeared as the restaurant menu expanded, siding replaced the building's limestone exterior (but limestone walls remain inside), and the business almost got torn down to make room for condominium development. That's when the Popes stepped in.

"I never dreamed we would own this place," says Chico, who also was raised in the neighborhood. He had longtime food industry experience. Dawn's expertise included bartending. They were ready to work for themselves instead of other people.

With the 1997 property purchase came longtime recipes, including a secret spice blend for prime rib. Now son Kevin is the head chef and daughter Shelley Huhnke handles front-of-the-house matters.

Evenings of business—Friday, Saturday, and Sunday—stayed the same, but now the Buckhorn also is open on Thursday night in summer and for brunch on Sunday. Live lobster boils happen outdoors on the last Tuesday and Wednesday of the month, May through October. The crustaceans are flown in from Maine, ninety are boiled at once and it's not unusual to run out.

One price covers a Caesar salad, the lobster, baby red potatoes, sweet corn, an array of desserts, and wine from Northleaf Winery, six miles away. Dinner is eaten as a keyboardist plays and sings easy-listening music; as the night unfolds, so does the likelihood of sing-alongs and dancing.

"We take great pride in being independent restaurant owners and a family-run business," Chico says. "We are committed to having someone from the family here whenever we are open." Dawn adds, "We get to know our customers—you are not just a number here."

Michelin-starred Chef Michael White, a native of Beloit, Wisconsin, is co-owner of The Butterfly Cocktails and Supper Club at 225 W. Broadway in Manhattan's Tribeca area. The restaurant opened in 2013, is part of the Altamarea Group of restaurants, and is named after a supper club in his hometown, which began as a tearoom in 1924. It is thirty miles south of The Buckhorn.

The chef worked as a cook at Beloit's Butterfly and in 2010 made the cut as Crain's New York Business "40 Most Influential New Yorkers Under 40." On the New York City's Butterfly menu: fried chicken dinners with honey butter biscuits, Swedish meatballs with cranberry jam, battered cheddar cheese curds, BLT salad, and more. thebutterflynyc.com, (646) 692-4943; butterflyclub.us, (608) 362-8577

The Buckhorn purchases thirty-pound containers of tart Montmorency cherries that are *[fro]*zen in their own juice, and grown in Wisconsin's Door County. This longtime favorite *[is]* great on roast duck, and leftover sauce can be refrigerated. Don't drain the cherries d*[uring]* preparation.

CHERRY SAUCE

Combine cherries with juice, 3 cups water, and sugar in a saucepan and bring to a boil. In a small bowl, mix cornstarch with 2 tablespoons water. Slowly mix into cherry mixture. Mix in chicken base. Return to a boil.

MAKES 1½ QUARTS

3 cups cherries, with juice
3 cups water
1¼ cups sugar, or to taste
⅓ cup cornstarch
2 tablespoons water
¼ teaspoon chicken base

This mustard-nut sauce, developed by Chico Pope, accompanies tilapia at The Buckhorn. It is an easy recipe to expand or reduce: The ideal proportions are two parts mayonnaise to one part mustard.

DIJON PECAN SAUCE

Preheat oven broiler. Mix mayonnaise and mustard. Spoon over baked fish. Top with pecans. Broil 1 to 2 minutes, or until sauce sets up (binds together).

MAKES 1 CUP

½ cup mayonnaise
¼ cup Dijon mustard
½ cup pecans

COLONY HOUSE RESTAURANT

25811 119th Street, Trevor
(262) 862-2076
colonyhouserestaurantwi.com
Owners: Eugene and Karen Stevens, Bruce and Lisa Francart

One mile north of the Wisconsin–Illinois border is a two-story house whose supper club feels like home. You also might feel the tension of football Sunday because the Colony House welcomes NFL fans from both states. "Go Pack Go!" says one guest book entry. "Go Bears!" shows up on the same page.

"There's a little rivalry here," acknowledges Karen Stevens, but this is no sports bar and repeat customers tend to also know each other as friends. She books, greets, and seats customers; husband Eugene cooks; brother-in-law Bruce handles cleanup and book work.

The Colony House sits where a shack housed seasonal workers for a sugar beet farm one century ago, until Phillip Lebandowski bought two acres and the building around 1920. He and a local milkman turned the structure into a larger and more substantial home that had a tavern below two rooms. He called the business Phil's Tavern and Café, serving low-alcohol beer, sandwiches, and a weekly fish fry.

The business, under different ownership, was the Rock Lake Tavern until Bill and Margaret Hovens took over in the 1940s. They rebuilt the structure with timbers from old stockyards in Trevor and were thoughtful about furnishings, which included thirteen barstools to represent the original thirteen colonies of the United States. The Hovens gave the supper club in this unincorporated community its present name; some of the barstools and other antiques are still around but not used.

Ownership changed two more times before the Stevens and Francarts took over in 1995. They aim to preserve

history while modernizing restaurant operations. The main dining room feels like a friend's home because of the fireplace and photos on the walls, and some dining tables are distinctive (they were used during the speakeasy days of Prohibition, made for poker games and designed with little spaces to store guns). In the basement is another fireplace and dining area with a private bar.

The supper club would have gained an outdoor gazebo in the late 1980s, but a building permit request was denied. There still is much more farmland than residential housing in the neighborhood, but corn and soybeans are harvested today, not sugar beets.

An appetizer of rumaki at the Colony House means a skewer of five broiled, bacon-wrapped chicken livers and water chestnuts. Veal cutlets are sautéed in red wine with mushrooms and tomatoes, sautéed with white wine with lemon and capers, or breaded and topped with mozzarella and a red sauce. A quartet of "Oscars"—filet mignon, chicken, veal, and salmon—are each topped with asparagus, king crab meat, and béarnaise sauce.

This is all in addition to traditional supper club fare, dinners that include soup, salad, a potato, and—on request, for no extra charge—honey-glazed carrots with onions. "They hold up well," Karen explains. "We used to give them to everybody but didn't like the waste" if they went uneaten.

The Colony House serves rumaki the old-time way, as bacon-wrapped chicken livers and water chestnuts. That combination dates back to the 1946 Trader Vic's Book of Food and Drink, whose recipe for the then-unusual combination included a dunking of the livers in "soya sauce" before being wrapped and fried. "Chicken Livers with Water Chestnuts" was the recipe title, but that changed in the 1968 Trader Vic's Pacific Island Cookbook, where the appetizer was called rumaki and spiced up with a marinade of ginger, star anise, garlic, cinnamon, and sugar.

"Trader Vic," aka Victor J. Bergeron, is known for introducing to California—and beyond—during the 1930s his version of tropical food and cocktails. How did he describe his unusual appetizer in 1946? "I'm going to give you just a few canapés and hors d'oeuvres which I think are interesting, which I know taste good and which won't aggravate someone's pet ulcer," his cookbook announced.

Today the restaurants of Trader Vic's Worldwide continue to embrace exotic cuisines and is known as Home of the Original Mai Tai. tradervics.com, (925) 675-6400

Customers rave about spinach salad at the Colony House because of the hot bacon dressing, which Eugene considers "a true, old supper club favorite." This version is simple to make, and leftovers can be refrigerated "for many meals to come. All you need to do is reheat it when needed."

HOT BACON DRESSING

1 pound bacon
1 Spanish onion
1 cup white vinegar
1 cup apple cider vinegar
2 cups cold water, divided
1 cup sugar
¼ cup cornstarch

Dice bacon and onion. Fry bacon in a large saucepan until nicely browned. Add onion and cook until onion is translucent. Strain off bacon grease.

In same saucepan, add vinegar, apple cider vinegar, 1 cup water, and sugar to bacon-onion mix. Bring to a boil.

In a small bowl, mix cornstarch and 1 cup water. Add, a little at a time, to boiling bacon mixture until thickened to desired consistency. Not all of the cornstarch mixture may be needed.

Serve over fresh spinach and whatever else sounds good, such as thinly sliced red onions and sliced hard-boiled eggs.

MAKES 1 QUART

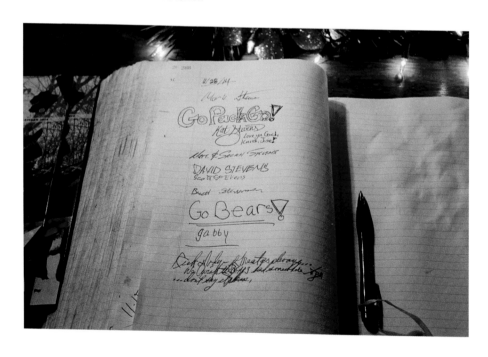

THE DEL-BAR

800 Wisconsin Dells Parkway, Lake Delton
(608) 253-1861
del-bar.com
Owners: Jeff and Jane Wimmer

The Del-Bar serves its meals Prairie style, and that especially is a big draw for some architecture buffs. James Dresser, a student of Frank Lloyd Wright who died in 2011, is the guy responsible for the 1952, 1963, and 1990 expansions and upgrades that give this supper club its signature style. Clean lines in design, furnishings, and lighting all show off the Prairie School architecture that remains a Wright trademark.

When built in the 1930s, the Del-Bar was not much more than a simple roadhouse situated halfway between the communities of Wisconsin Dells and Baraboo serving charcoal-broiled steaks. The name Del-Bar and location remain, even though owners have changed and what used to be rural now is a major thoroughfare that is awash with water parks, other tourist attractions, lodging, and restaurants.

Jeff's parents, Jimmy and Alice Wimmer, borrowed five hundred dollars from a friend and took over the Del-Bar in 1943. Count that friend's family among the Del-Bar's loyal customers for four generations. Now the restaurant is at least five times its original size; the Garden Room was the supper club's first dining room.

"The architecture will never change," says Jane Wimmer, Jeff's wife. "Those lines are its strength." Although quality cuts of beef remain a key component of the menu, "we are a new-fashioned steakhouse. I don't want us to feel old" in looks or dining choices. "We have a sophisticated style here—contemporary and spacious."

Prime, aged steaks and pan-fried walleye are longtime Chef Mike Uptagraw's top entrees, but what really helps separate the food choices from

most other supper clubs is the oyster bar menu, which dates back to the 1960s. "Nobody in this area got fresh seafood back then, but we were on the route from a Chicago distributor and would get the last three boxes" on the delivery route, Jane says.

Her in-laws would get these wild ideas about what to serve during research visits to Chicago, especially when at The Drake Hotel. The hotel's Cape Cod Room kitchen is where they got an introduction to fresh oysters and clam chowder, and where they learned how to source and order seafood. Chef Henri de Jonghe, in Chicago's Loop, shared recipes for baked onion soup and his signature Shrimp de Jonghe.

Today the Del-Bar usually serves two kinds of oysters from the East Coast and one from the West Coast. Jane says the difference in taste is brine (for East Coast choices) versus mineral. "It's definitely two different flavors—the terroir makes a difference," she explains. "Oysters are as complicated as wine" (and the Del-Bar has earned Wine Spectator awards routinely since the 1990s).

Architect Frank Lloyd Wright has left his mark in Wisconsin in all kinds of ways. Fifty miles south of Wisconsin Dells is the Taliesin estate where he lived and worked for forty-eight years. Seasonal tours of Taliesin attract thousands every year, and the site is one of two Wright sites in Wisconsin and one of ten in the United States that are on track to be designated as a World Heritage Site. taliesinpreservation.org, (877) 588-7900

You could say that the uplands of southwest Wisconsin, especially the curvy and woodsy Wyoming Valley, were Wright's roots and wings. In and near the artsy community of Spring Green are inspirations for the legendary architect's design principles.

The simple quarters of his summer boyhood playground, Aldebaran Farm—near his family's Unity Chapel, are rented to groups for overnight stays. More than one dozen other structures pertinent to Wright's life or designs are within a short drive. springgreen.com, (608) 588-2054

The Del-Bar has stayed true to this longtime recipe for oysters, which remains an unusual (but not unprecedented) appetizer choice for supper clubs today.

OYSTERS ROCKEFELLER

1 cup butter
¾ cup diced uncooked bacon
1½ cups chopped green onion
1 cup chopped parsley
2½ teaspoons Tabasco
2 ounces anisette
1 cup heavy cream
36 fresh oysters on half shells
1 cup shredded Havarti cheese

Melt butter. Set aside. Fry bacon and cool. Mix all ingredients except oysters and cheese in a large bowl. Refrigerate.

Preheat oven to 450°F. Spoon mixture over oysters, just filling the shells. Top each with Havarti cheese. Bake 5 minutes, then broil briefly until cheese is golden.

SERVES 9–12

DORF HAUS SUPPER CLUB

8931 Highway Y, Sauk City
(608) 643-3980
foodspot.com
Owners: Rebecca Maier-Frey and Monte Maier

Monday typically is a slow night for restaurants, and supper clubs are no exception. Most owners take the day off, but that's not always how it works at Dorf Haus. The only place bigger than this supper club in the little town of Sauk City, population eighteen hundred, is St. Norbert's Catholic Church (just across the street).

Dorf Haus hosts a Monday Smorgasbord at least monthly, and it turns into one big party. A polka band performs from an elevated stage, above the wooden dance floor where some diners linger to burn off a few calories. On the buffet are Bavarian favorites: schnitzels, sauerbraten, schweinsrippen, knackwurst, pork hocks, spaetzle, kraut, salads, and desserts. The music ends before 9 p.m., so it's not a late night out.

Roxbury was settled by German immigrants, and Dorf Haus—the village inn—is here because of Vern and Betty Maier, parents of Rebecca, Monte, and seven other children. Vern and Betty's wedding reception was at this location in 1950, when the building was a small dance hall, bar, and grocery store. Before the decade ended, they bought the place.

"They were going to run a mill shop in the back of the building, and a bar in the front," says Rebecca. Her father, a farmer, went to an auction to buy compressors, only to find them packaged with restaurant equipment. Why not give it a try? Their restaurant began in 1961 as a nook serving one-dollar family-style chicken dinners on weekends to twenty-five people at a time. Now the special, still served on Friday, is offered in a building that seats up to 450. (More than 700 dine during the Thanksgiving buffet.)

Popular appetizers are chicken livers and Reuben balls, but traditional supper club favorites hold their own, too. Senior citizens and kids have lighter-fare choices. Lenten Fridays are "turtle time"—turtle meat is marinated with carrots and onions overnight, roasted four hours, and served with mashed potatoes, gravy, coleslaw, and fritters. Taste and texture resemble roast beef.

Vern Maier began the turtle tradition in the 1980s, to provide his pious Catholic customers with an option to fish. Orders are phoned in advance, so

supply matches demand, because this annual novelty is popular. It's simply coincidence that turtle cheesecake is the top-selling Dorf Haus dessert.

Indoors are German antiques, stained glass panes, paintings of castles, leaded glass windows, ornate furnishings, and murals of faraway places. In the backyard is a gazebo and garden, which makes Dorf Haus a popular spot for weddings.

Vern and Betty died twenty-one days apart in 2012, knowing that Catholics still walked over for a meal after Mass, that farmers made time for afternoons of oompah music, and that their offspring were devoted to carrying on family traditions. "*Gemuetlich* at its best," is how Rebecca describes it.

By 1880 14 percent of Wisconsin residents were German-born, and it was the highest such concentration in the country. So many settled here because of fertile farmland and rural landscapes that were comforting reminders of home.

More people in Wisconsin claimed German ancestry in the 2010 US Census than any other state. That translated to almost 2.5 million people, or 43 percent of the state's population.

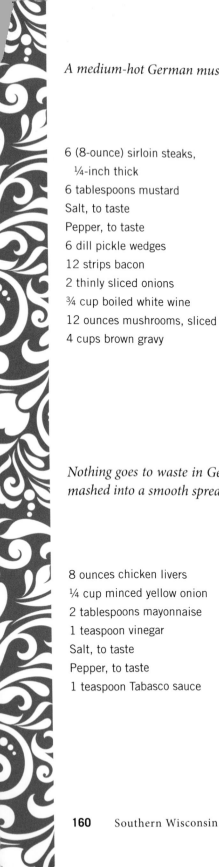

A medium-hot German mustard is recommended for this classic German recipe.

BEEF ROULADEN

6 (8-ounce) sirloin steaks,
  ¼-inch thick
6 tablespoons mustard
Salt, to taste
Pepper, to taste
6 dill pickle wedges
12 strips bacon
2 thinly sliced onions
¾ cup boiled white wine
12 ounces mushrooms, sliced
4 cups brown gravy

Preheat oven to 350°F. Place steaks on a flat surface and spread a thin layer of mustard on each one. Season with salt and pepper.

Place one pickle wedge at one end of each steak. Place two bacon strips near the center of each steak. Cover bacon strips with onion slices.

Starting at the pickle end, tightly roll steaks. Do not push out bacon or onion slices. Place rolled meat into a baking pan that is at least 4 inches deep.

Add wine to pan. Combine mushrooms and gravy in a bowl. Pour over beef rolls. Cover and cook 3 to 3½ hours, or until meat is tender.

SERVES 6

Nothing goes to waste in German cooking, and that includes chicken livers, which are cooked and mashed into a smooth spread for crackers.

LIVER PÂTÉ

8 ounces chicken livers
¼ cup minced yellow onion
2 tablespoons mayonnaise
1 teaspoon vinegar
Salt, to taste
Pepper, to taste
1 teaspoon Tabasco sauce

Boil livers until tender. Drain and cool.

Blend livers and onions in food processor until smooth. Move to a small mixing bowl.

In a separate bowl mix mayonnaise, vinegar, salt, and pepper. Add to liver mixture until consistency is firm but wet. Add Tabasco sauce.

SERVES 6–8

THE EDGEWATER SUPPER CLUB

N3522 Highway K, Jefferson
(920) 674-9942
theedgewatersupperclub.com
Owners: Vicki and Bill Millis

Customers get to The Edgewater by car, foot, bicycle, canoe, kayak, and, occasionally, plane. In that latter group are The Flying Farmers, private pilots who fill a round table at this supper club monthly.

Fort Atkinson Municipal Airport is across the road and so is the Wisconsin Skydiving Center, whose student jumps are an unusual sideshow for before-dark diners during summer. "You can see them jump and watch their techniques," Vicki Millis says. "We make little bets about which one will land first or stay up the longest."

It's all in good fun, and the view is prime from The Edgewater's outdoor tables for casual lounging. Dining happens inside, where the greeter likely is Vicki's dad, Blaine Adams. He also is the guy who refinished the twenty-two-foot-long mahogany bar.

The 1911 building doesn't look flashy from the outside, but inside are unique little gems. Above a fireplace hearth are the words *hearth* and *cheer*. On some tabletops are one-of-a-kind centerpieces, dried flower arrangements to a softly lit stained glass lantern.

Favorite spots for diners are two private nooks and an enclosed porch with tables that overlook the Rock River. Time it right, and you'll see fluttering hummingbirds or fish jumping out of the water. In mid-spring, pelicans call this terrain their home for a while. Five miles northwest is Hi-Way 18, one of Wisconsin's increasingly rare drive-in movie theaters.

The Millis family reopened The Edgewater in 2013, after it was shuttered for almost three years. They also operate Under the Oaks Farm, which raises organic vegetables, pastured chickens, and ring neck pheasants at the edge of Kettle Moraine State Forest. Vicki is in charge of cooking, and Bill usually bartends. Sister Joy Adams, daughter Sarah Davis, and grandson Chase Davis also play key roles in the supper club's operation.

This is a family that proceeds in unconventional ways because "eating local" and "farm to table" are not just fashionable phrases. Consider how they introduce themselves online:

> The classic supper club offerings of steaks and seafood may resemble your favorite menu items from past Edgewater experiences, but under the new ownership of the Millis family the care and ethic behind the menu choices are distinctly different. We pride ourselves on offering the best locally raised products, making personal connections with the farmers who raise our food, and supporting the local economy in the choices we make as a restaurant.

When the daily special is chicken, the poultry comes from Under the Oaks. Steaks come from Neesvig's, forty miles northwest and in business since 1913. Other regional vendors are listed online routinely. Vicki makes her own "farm recipe" sausages; her fresh sauerkraut, marmalades, and kombucha are sold by the pint in a retail space that will grow in size to accommodate the honey, maple syrup, and other products of neighborhood farms. Some customers order frozen chicken, after a meal, to prepare later in their own kitchens.

The bar already stocks craft beer and small-batch spirits made in Wisconsin, but plans don't end there. The Edgewater bottled its first batch of sparkling wine, their version of Cold Duck, to welcome the arrival of 2015. Next comes the development of tasty but unpredictable, non-alcoholic, and—as Vicki puts it, "better for you"—beverages. That project acknowledges the stricter enforcement of drunk-driving laws in recent years.

Personal attention to customer concerns doesn't stop there. Consider the couple who decided to walk more than three miles to the supper club. Online, they said Bill "fetched us a reflector vest from the basement" before they began the walk home in the dark. "He said he couldn't afford to lose good customers to roadkill. We are happy to say that we live to eat another day."

Don and Angeline Millis, Bill's parents, operated a hunting preserve from the 1940s to 1970s and decades ago came up with this recipe, which The Edgewater uses today. Note: If the birds are farm raised (not a hunter's wild bounty), it is not necessary to soak them in the vinegar-water mix mentioned below.

FESTIVE PHEASANT

For the marinade:

½ cup cooking oil

¼ cup lemon juice

Dash of oregano

Dash of onion salt

2 tablespoons soy sauce

1 tablespoon Worcestershire
  sauce

1 teaspoon salt

1 teaspoon pepper

¼ teaspoon thyme

For the poultry:

4 pheasants

1 quart water, or more

1 quart vinegar, or more

Cooking oil or butter, as
  needed

½ cup sweet red wine

3 (10.75-ounce) cans cream
  of chicken soup

½ cup water

For the gravy:

Roasting pan juices

2 tablespoons cornstarch

2 tablespoons cold water

Mix marinade ingredients. Set aside.

Disjoint the birds and trim off excess fat. If wild game, soak in a 50-50 mix of vinegar and water for 1 hour. Drain and place cut-up birds in a 9 x 13 x 2-inch baking pan. If two pans are needed, make twice as much marinade.

Pour the marinade over the pheasant and turn pieces several times to coat. Cover and refrigerate overnight.

Preheat oven to 250°F. Remove pheasant from marinade. Pat dry before quickly frying the birds in butter or cooking oil. Place pheasant in a roasting pan.

To the drippings left in the frying pan, add wine to deglaze. Blend in soup and water, stirring over low heat. Pour mixture over pheasant in roasting pan. Cover with foil and roast 5 to 6 hours, until fall-off-the-bone tender.

Remove pheasant and keep warm. Move roasting pan to medium-high heat on stovetop. Mix cornstarch and cold water. Add to roasting pan juices, stirring until thickened into gravy.

SERVES 8

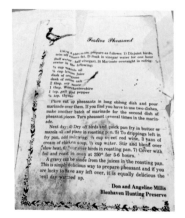

A buttery base enriches this supper club soup, which turns into a vegetarian offer
ing vegetable stock or water for the chicken stock. The flavor ranges from slightly sw
depending on the type of Hungarian paprika used.

HUNGARIAN MUSHROOM SOUP

Sauté onions in 2 tablespoons butter. Salt lightly. Add mushrooms, dill weed, ½ cup stock or water, tamari or soy sauce, and paprika. Cover and simmer 15 minutes.

Melt remaining butter in a large saucepan. Whisk in flour and cook briefly. Add milk and then cook, stir frequently, over low heat for 10 minutes or until thick. Stir in mushroom mixture and remaining stock or water. Cover and simmer 10 to 15 minutes.

Just before serving, add remaining salt, pepper, sour cream, optional lemon juice, and, if desired, extra dill. Garnish with parsley.

SERVES 4–5

2 cups chopped onion
4 tablespoons butter, divided
1 teaspoon salt, divided
12 ounces sliced fresh
  mushrooms
2 teaspoons dill weed
2 cups chicken stock or water,
  divided
1 tablespoon tamari or soy sauce
1 tablespoon Hungarian paprika
3 tablespoons flour
1 cup milk
½ teaspoon pepper
½ cup sour cream
2 teaspoons fresh lemon juice,
  optional
¼ cup fresh chopped parsley

HOBNOB

277 S. Sheridan Road, Racine
(262) 552-8008
thehobnob.com
Owners: Mike Aletto and Anne Glowacki

All kinds of big and small details turn the HobNob into an extraordinary supper club. The location is a once-rural shoreline of Lake Michigan, at the half-way point between Racine and Kenosha. How close is the water? Close enough for parking lot signs to playfully warn, Stop Lake Michigan Ahead. It's a can't-miss business because of neon signage and a gigantic martini painted on the front of the building.

Inside is a lush and over-the-top mix of Naugahyde white booths and bar seats, heavy and fringed drapes, silken wall fabrics, purple ceilings, and intimate dining areas that are dramatic in appearance. The style resembles art deco. Under glass is a 1950s menu, back when a shorty beer was thirty cents, a slice of cheesecake thirty-five cents, and a shrimp cocktail one dollar. Almost all of the house specialties—prime rib, roasted duckling, barbecued ribs, thick lamb chops, and one-pound pork chops—remain on the menu. The $3.50 steamed Finnan haddie, smoked haddock named after a town in Scotland, has vanished.

"They're driving far to come to us and coming for a particular entree," Mike Aletto says, "so we don't have to change a lot." He and wife Anne Glowacki have owned the supper club since 1990 and now live in Florida, but they return to the HobNob at least monthly. They bought it from Bill Higgins Jr., son of the original owners, Bill and Belle Higgins, who opened it as Higgins' HobNob in 1954. From 1937 to 1941, Higgins' HobNob was in downtown Racine, five miles north of its present site.

"We're a place to come to enjoy a whole evening—this is your night out," Mike says. "Miss Lillian," a cabaret-style piano player, has entertained in the Lakeview Terrace lounge on Saturday night since the mid-1990s. A trio of musicians adds soft jazz on Friday. Diners used to pay fifty cents for access to rooftop dancing and cocktails during summer, until a change in fire safety codes ended the practice.

Now Lakeview Terrace is where people linger, and dessert means ice-cream drinks. "As soon as one is paraded through the dining room, everybody orders them," says Kara Wunderle, special events coordinator. The supper club has no television sets, which means business historically is quiet during Green Bay Packer game time, but the HobNob has not served lunch for many years.

Although the Moroccan Room can seat up to six, it's informally nicknamed the "footsie room" because it's more likely to be reserved by a couple for a special meal that occasionally involves a marriage proposal. After that happens, Kara says, chances are good they'll request the same seating, sometimes every year. "There are a lot of memories in this room," she acknowledges.

An eclectic assortment of luminaries—architect Frank Lloyd Wright, filmmaker Walt Disney, singer Patti Page, radio broadcaster Paul Harvey, football players LeRoy Butler and Charles Woodson—has dined at the HobNob. TV host Steve Allen was the first person to sign the guest book.

Now younger generations are taking a taste of supper club style. "Thirty-year-olds are loving different food experiences such as this," Kara says. "They love being in a place different than the chain" restaurants. She mentions a couple who hired Rat Pack impersonators for their wedding reception, and groups who organize supper club tours as a vacation. It's all good, as long as they expect a leisurely pace because "for people who want to be in and out in forty-five minutes, we have a hard time doing it."

Mike Aletto calls his supper club's longtime duck recipe "a German-style classic for th[...]
still is ordered frequently. Stuff the bird with whatever type of dressing you prefer. [...]
to be generous.

ROASTED DUCKLING A LA ORANGE

Preheat oven to 500°F. Rinse ducklings inside and out. Pat dry. Fill cavity with dressing. Secure cavity opening with wooden skewers and string. Brush skin with oil.

Generously season ducklings with salt, pepper, and paprika. Rub these seasonings all over the ducklings, working them into the skin.

Place birds in shallow pan and add ½ inch of water. Bake uncovered for 30 minutes. Lower temperature to 350°F and bake 2½ to 3 hours longer. Cover lightly with aluminum foil if skin becomes too crisp.

For sauce, cut orange into four wedges. Do not peel. Remove seeds and membrane from red and yellow peppers. Cut into strips.

Place oranges, peppers, and orange juice in a saucepan. Bring to a boil. Simmer until peppers soften. Remove from heat.

Remove orange wedges. Pour remaining ingredients into a blender. Blend well, then strain.

Return strained mixture to saucepan. Add honey and sugar. Mix and simmer until sugar dissolves. If needed to thicken, mix cornstarch with an equal portion of cold water. Add to sauce.

To serve, remove wooden skewers and string from ducklings. Cut ducklings in half, lengthwise. Place each piece, cut side down, on a plate. Top with warmed orange sauce.

SERVES 4

For the duckling:
2 (4.5- or 5-pound) ducklings
5 cups sage dressing
4 tablespoons canola oil
Salt, to taste
Pepper, to taste
4 teaspoons paprika

For the sauce:
1 orange
½ red pepper
½ yellow pepper
8 cups orange juice
¼ cup plus 1 tablespoon honey
¼ cup plus 1 tablespoon sugar
Pinch of cornstarch, if needed to
  thicken

HOUSE OF EMBERS

935 Wisconsin Dells Parkway, Wisconsin Dells
(608) 253-6411
houseofembers.com
Owners: Mike Obois and Deb Christensen

What is more intimate in dining than a table for two? Try a room for two. That is the draw of the Omar Sharif Room at House of Embers; what started as a coatroom has turned into the site of around five hundred marriage proposals. On walls of the tiny space are framed photos and posters from the actor's best-known movies: *Doctor Zhivago*, *Funny Girl*, *Lawrence of Arabia*, and more. Drapes at the nook's entry are drawn to add privacy.

Slightly larger are the Rudolph Valentino Room, a former alcohol storage nest, and the Humphrey Bogart Room, a private alcove. All add to the ambiance

of the neon-glow supper club, whose larger dining areas gain distinction from a Ben Franklin stove, a two-sided fireplace, Tiffany lighting, and enclosed porch seating. Light jazz or pop music plays in the spacious circular lounge.

What we have is a big contrast to Ray's Barbecue, a two-room barbecue shack with a dirt basement, which is what was cooking here until 1959, when Wally and Barbara Obois joined a temporary partner to buy and reposition the property, literally and figuratively. A decision to smoke spareribs over embers of charcoal is what inspired the new name, and hickory-smoked ribs continues as a House of Embers specialty. Another draw is Barbara's cinnamon rolls,

When the Oboises built a new supper club, it was behind the original building, which was razed. Business closed for only two weeks during the 1976 transition, and that was to move from one building to the other. Since the owners' retirement in 1998, daughter Deb Christensen and son Mike Obois run the show. He is trained chef, a graduate of the Culinary Institute of America, and his sister's college degree in finance makes her an ideal manager of business details.

The addition of an outdoor area for eating and drinking in 2011 adds a casual element to an otherwise special-occasion destination. Like its menu and decor, House of Embers is a mix of tradition and the unexpected. So order deep-fried cheese curds as an appetizer, or splurge on the seafood martini (lobster, shrimp, and a sweet chile lime aioli) that is big enough to share. For dessert: hot fudge sundaes, chocolate caramel toffee cake, lemon meringue ice-cream pie, or the cheesecake of the day.

Serve this classic dressing with wedges of iceberg lettuce. At House of Embers, that means o[...] of a lettuce head per serving and each wedge doused with dressing. Garnish with wa[...] bacon; House of Embers prefers Wisconsin-based Nueske's bacon.

BLUE CHEESE DRESSING

Stir all ingredients together. Do not overmix.

SERVES 4–6

1½ cups crumbled blue cheese
½ teaspoon fresh lemon juice
1 tablespoon Worcestershire sauce
2½ cups sour cream
¾ teaspoon salt
½ teaspoon pepper
½ teaspoon garlic salt

Wisconsin Dells calls itself the Water Park Capital of the World and says the Polynesian Resort was the nation's first indoor water park in 1989. Now the area claims to have the most indoor/outdoor water park configurations per capita.

That includes America's largest outdoor water park (the 70-acre Noah's Ark Water Park), the largest indoor/outdoor water park (500,000 square feet at Wilderness Hotel and Golf Resort), and at least 200 waterslides. wisdells.com, (800) 223-3557

Garnish this lovely dessert with dollops of whipped cream and fresh fruit. The dessert is a favorite of Clair Obois, Mike's daughter, who got her first taste of it in 2004, at age three, and maintains no other rendition comes close.

WHITE CHOCOLATE CHEESECAKE

For the crust:

1½ cups crushed graham
   crackers

¼ cup melted butter

For the cheesecake:

18 ounces (2¼ cups) white
   chocolate

½ cup heavy whipping cream

3½ (8-ounce) packages
   softened cream cheese

1 cup sugar

1 teaspoon salt

6 eggs

1½ teaspoons vanilla

Whipped cream

Fresh fruit

Thoroughly combine graham crackers and melted butter. Press into the bottom of a 9-inch springform pan. Set aside.

Preheat oven to 350°F. Stir chocolate and cream over low heat until melted. Set aside.

Mix cream cheese, sugar, and salt. Add eggs, one at a time, scraping the sides of the bowl as needed. Paddle in white chocolate mixture and vanilla. Pour into graham cracker crust.

Bake 60 minutes, or until set. Cool, garnish with whipped cream and fruit, and serve.

SERVES 8–10

JOEY GERARD'S: A BARTOLOTTA SUPPER CLUB

5601 Broad Street, Greendale
(414) 858-1900
11120 N. Cedarburg Road, Mequon
(262) 518-5500
joeygerards.com
Owner: Joe Bartolotta

One of the Milwaukee area's most respected and award-winning restaurant groups is the Bartolotta Restaurants, established in 1993 with the opening of Ristorante Bartolotta, whose menu remains a tribute to the Italian roots of founders Joe and Paul Bartolotta. The brothers, with sisters Maria and Felicia, grew up in the Milwaukee suburb of Wauwatosa.

What began as one restaurant with traditional Italian fare, including pasta made by hand, has expanded to a portfolio of distinctly different dining concepts in a dozen locations. That includes a custard and burger stand on the shore of Lake Michigan to fine dining at Bacchus, which boasts a wine menu of at least 750 choices.

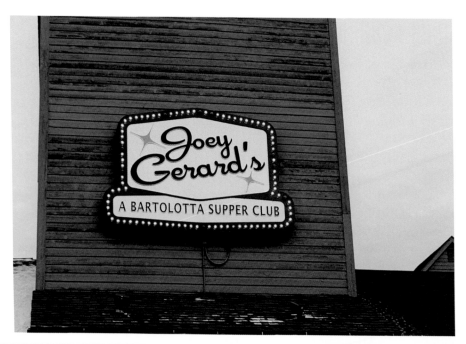

Joey Gerard's opened in 2012 and has two suburban Milwaukee locations that opened within two months of each other. The supper clubs are a tribute to the owner's parents, Tudy and Beverly Bartolotta, and the dining is all about nostalgia and comfort. "When his mom meant business, she would call him by his first and middle names—Joey Gerard," says executive chef Andrew Ruiz, to explain the business name.

The setting at both locations is more about old-time Hollywood glamour than rural, small-town Wisconsin. Above dark leather booths hang black-and-white photographs of celebrities dining and imbibing in the 1930s to 1970s. You'll see Ronald Reagan and Jane Wyman at the Brown Derby in Los Angeles in 1940, Marlene Dietrich and Rita Hayworth at the Hollywood Canteen in 1944. A brochure maps out who's who and where in each of the fifty photos.

Menus include Friday fish specials (beer-battered cod or pan-fried perch) and Maine lobster stuffed with crab on Friday and Saturday. To-go options include a sautéed calf's liver with a sauce of red currants and pearl onions. A menu just for ages under twelve includes the Kid's Steak, a top sirloin with mashed potatoes, plus an ice-cream sundae.

"When we created the menu, we wanted the items to be classically prepared. We didn't stray, or put our twist on anything. We do pride ourselves with the fact that everything we make is from scratch. Nothing is brought in premade, and we source as much produce as we can from a family farm" in the area, says chef Andrew.

Dinner customers automatically receive a relish tray of carrots, celery, green onion stalks, black olives, and Green Goddess dressing for dipping. More nibbles come from ordering The Lazy Susan, whose assortment might include deviled eggs, summer sausage, a cheese ball, and/or smoked whitefish.

The cocktail menu encourages visitors to "drink like it's 1958," which means considering an adult milk shake like Pal Joey, a combination of Kahlua, Bailey's Irish Cream, Amaretto, crème de cacao, mascarpone, and ice cream. This is in addition to classic and craft cocktails.

Andrew says all meats cook in a specialized coal-fired oven-grill that, when set about seven hundred degrees, imparts a smoky, charred flavor. He works under the direction of Corporate Chef Adam Siegel, who was deemed Best Chef Midwest by the James Beard Foundation in 2008 for his work at Bartolotta's Lake Park Bistro. Paul Bartolotta has earned two Beard awards: 1994 Best Chef Midwest, while at Chicago's Spiaggia, and 2009 Best Chef Southwest, for Bartolotta's Ristorante di Mare at the Wynn Hotel in Las Vegas.

Wisconsinites long ago affectionately began referring to this little treat as a "cannibal sandw... *steak tartare. The seasoned raw beef was traditionally popular on New Year's Eve buffets, a... the top appetizer at Joey Gerard's. Use a high-quality beef that is freshly ground, Andrew advi... not use store-bought ground beef in a package. Ask your local butcher to grind the meat, or bu... own meat grinder. The aggressive mixing of meat with seasonings (Lawry's is the preferred seasoned salt) plays a key role in accentuating the final flavor and texture.*

RAW BEEF AND ONIONS

Combine ground beef, olive oil, kosher salt, seasoned salt, and pepper in a chilled mixing bowl. Mix fairly aggressively with a fork, and whip until the beef starts to look slightly creamy.

Serve cold, accompanied by slices of onion and rye bread. Add a small spreading knife, so guests can build a sandwich as thick or thin as they desire. Make extra seasoned salt available, too.

SERVES 4

5 ounces ground beef
(tenderloin, eye of round)
2 tablespoons extra virgin olive
oil
¼ teaspoon kosher salt
½ teaspoon seasoned salt
¼ teaspoon freshly cracked
black pepper
Sliced yellow onion
Cocktail rye bread

In the Purple Door Ice Cream line, introduced by Lauren and Steve Schultz in 2011, is the Brandy Old-Fashioned flavor of ice cream. Purple Door began as a Milwaukee wholesale business and added a retail location that serves twenty flavors in the Walker's Point neighborhood of Milwaukee.

"The idea was out there for a long time," Steve says of the Brandy Old-Fashioned flavor. "After our whiskey flavor came out, we started getting requests from customers" about adding an old-fashioned flavor. "Before putting it to the public, we went through many trials and across the palates of countless hard-core old-fashioned drinkers."

The next step is to make it a standard flavor that is available in grocery stores. purpledooricecream.com, (414) 988-2521

This classic entree tastes great over cooked egg noodles or German spaetzle (tiny dumplings).

BEEF STROGANOFF

5 pounds beef stew meat
Salt, to taste
Pepper, to taste
¼ cup corn oil
½ tablespoon garlic puree
5 springs fresh thyme
1 bay leaf
¼ cup tomato paste
2 quarts chicken stock
2 tablespoons butter,
  divided
½ pound pearl onions
1½ pounds button
  mushrooms
¼ cup Dijon mustard
3 cups sour cream

Season meat with salt and pepper. Heat corn oil in skillet. Add meat and sear over medium-high heat until all sides are browned. Add garlic puree, thyme, and bay leaf. Add tomato paste, stir, and cook a few minutes.

Add chicken stock, bring to a simmer, cover, and braise 1½ hours.

In a separate pan, melt 1 tablespoon butter over medium heat. Add onions and stir gently to coat. Reduce heat and stir occasionally until caramelized, about 30 minutes. Add to beef.

Cut mushrooms into quarters. Use the same skillet to caramelize the mushrooms with the remaining butter. Add to beef.

Add Dijon mustard to beef mixture and simmer uncovered until beef is tender. Fold in sour cream and bring mixture back to a simmer. Adjust seasoning.

SERVES 6–8

Serve this entree with a potato puree and garnish with chopped parsley. When the dish
the 1950s, Andrew notes, it was one of many tableside dishes popular at the time. A b
of the sauce would add "a bit of showmanship."

STEAK DIANE

Preheat oven to 400F. Season steaks with salt and pepper. Heat corn oil in 12-inch sauté pan and sear steaks over medium-high heat until both sides are browned.

Turn heat off. Transfer meat to a baking dish and place in oven until they are cooked to your liking (8 to 12 minutes).

Cut mushrooms into quarters. Melt butter in sauté pan used to sear steaks. Add mushrooms and cook over medium-high heat. Add shallot and garlic purees; cook until mushrooms are golden brown.

Add brandy and white wine to sauté pan. Be mindful to not ignite the alcohol. Stir and cook the liquid until it is almost gone. Add beef stock and mustard. Cook until reduced by half.

Add cream and cook until sauce is of a nice, creamy consistency. (It will coat the back of a spoon.) Stir in soy sauce and Worcestershire. Adjust seasoning. Spoon sauce over steaks.

6 (6-ounce) filet mignon
Salt, to taste
Pepper, to taste
¼ cup corn oil
12 ounces button mushrooms
2 tablespoons unsalted butter
1 teaspoon pureed shallot
1 teaspoon pureed garlic
½ cup brandy
½ cup dry white wine
1½ cups beef stock
2 tablespoons Dijon mustard
1½ cups heavy cream
2 teaspoons soy sauce
1 teaspoon Worcestershire sauce

SERVES 6

Kavanaugh's Esquire Club

1025 N. Sherman Avenue, Madison
(608) 249-0193
esquireclubmadison.com
Owners: John and Linda Kavanaugh

John Kavanaugh isn't known for his breakfasts, but one Saturday every December is an exception. When Santa visits, eight hundred kids and parents eat pancakes within three hours. Around fifty volunteers help make this happen, and proceeds benefit neighborhood food pantries.

Families bring toys to donate and wish lists for themselves. Hearing who wants what was John's job for a couple of years, until he realized there was no way for Santa to double as the supper club's troubleshooter. Other than that, playing Santa was a pretty good match because listening to what people need or want is a big part of both jobs.

John is three years younger than the Esquire Club, which parents Jack and Jane Kavanaugh opened in 1947 as a snug, fifty-by-fifty-foot box of a restaurant near the outskirts of Madison. The neighborhood has grown remarkably in size and diversity since then, just like the supper club.

A half a mile east is the Oscar Mayer meat products plant, which employs twelve hundred. About the same distance west is Maple Bluff's mansions and the Executive Residence, home to Wisconsin's governor. So Kavanaugh's is where blue and white collars, liberals and conservatives, retirees and young families blend under one roof in a dining room that seats seventy.

Success means coming up with a menu that suits people inclined to order a five-hundred-dollar bottle of wine and those on the lookout for happy hour bargains. It is a gallant attempt to define and seek opportunity, as the business logo—a cocktail-toting bovine with a fish tail—suggests. Steak? Seafood? Sandwich? Light lunch, or the full deal—with leftovers? All is possible here.

The restaurant's exterior is nothing extraordinary, but gradual upgrades expanded the bar, replaced the kitchen, added a thirty-seat private dining room and two banquet areas, each of which accommodates 120. A big challenge to growth is deciding how to uphold long-standing traditions while widening the number of dietary choices. Having a seven-ounce tenderloin and two-pound porterhouse on the menu doesn't cut enough of a range.

"You don't want to kick anybody to the curb, but you have to evolve," John says. "A rib eye (steak) is still a rib eye today, but we're offering more sandwich wraps and creative salads and gluten-free and vegetarian" options because that's what customers want. Loyalty, he knows, is easier to nurture when people know you're paying attention to details and customer preferences.

The hand dipping of onion rings into batter matters and prevails. So does serving three thousand pounds of corned beef during the week of St. Patrick's Day, guessing how much prime rib you'll need on a Saturday night and keeping liver and onions on the menu for senior citizens.

"People come here with expectations and get into a routine," John notes. "They might not eat these things at any other place or time of year." Loyal customers expect to taste the same coleslaw recipe and the same breading for fried fish.

"The good news is that we have regular customers," John says. "And the bad news is that we have regular customers," which means it's hard to drop anything from the menu. Some people dine at Kavanaugh's more than once a week. Retired firefighters and retired police officers gather for mini reunions. Groups of card players regularly meet here.

Being independently owned makes it easier to address customer requests. "We don't have to have a board meeting to make split pea soup or pork hocks and kraut the special in a couple of days, after somebody says they've been craving it," says the nine-year National Restaurant Association board member.

He bought the restaurant in 1978, when his father was sixty-two. Daughter Jackie and son Johnny ensure that Kavanaugh's will enter a third generation of business. "I kind of hope they figure out a way to kick me out," the father says. "In any family business, the kids need to really want to take over. If they just do it for their parents, they increase their chances of failure.

"We all know that restaurants come after gas, light, and rent. We are about entertainment and the customer's spare dollars."

A cook named Hilde in the 1960s introduced to Kavanaugh's this spread for crackers[...] featured daily since then and is a favorite of guests. Freshly grated cheeses make for a[...] sistency than shredded cheeses that are packaged. To make super-easy work of this re[...] a cold-pack cheddar for the shredded cheese, John Kavanaugh advises.

BEER AND CHEESE SPREAD

Combine cheeses, Worcestershire sauce, dry mustard, and garlic. Beat in enough beer to make spreading consistency. Serve on assorted crackers or rye bread.

MAKES 3 CUPS

2 cups shredded sharp cheddar cheese
2 cups shredded swiss cheese
1 teaspoon Worcestershire sauce
½ teaspoon dry mustard
1 small garlic clove, minced
½ to ⅔ cup beer

Spreadable cheese, also known as cold-pack cheese, has been popular for nearly a century, especially in supper club settings. Look for a scoop on a plate near or in the bar, surrounded by crackers and free for the taking.

Wisconsin taverns in the early 1900s provided the product as snack food for customers, reports *Cheese Market News*, a trade publication for the industry. Hubert Fassbender of Kaukauna Cheese gets credit as the person who perfected the cold-pack method of cheese production. The spread was sold in a ceramic crock and nicknamed "club cheese" in 1933. kaukaunacheese.com

The cheese spread is made by blending cheeses without using heat. A cousin is Velveeta, introduced in half-pound bricks as a smooth mix of aged cheddar and swiss by cheesemaker Emil Frey in Monroe, Wisconsin. Velveeta became a Kraft Foods product in 1927.

This recipe was a favorite of Jane Kavanaugh, the first generation to operate the supper club. Note that this is a no-bake dessert with raw eggs in the filling. If that makes you squeamish, John Kavanaugh suggests using pasteurized eggs.

MINT TORTE

¾ cup butter, divided

2 cups vanilla wafer crumbs

1½ cups powdered sugar

3 lightly beaten eggs

3 (1-ounce) squares
  unsweetened chocolate,
  melted

2 cups whipping cream

1 (10.5-ounce) package
  miniature marshmallows

½ cup crushed peppermint
  candy

Melt ¼ cup butter and blend with vanilla wafer crumbs. Press firmly into the bottom of a greased 8-inch-square pan. Cream together remaining butter and powdered sugar. Add eggs and melted chocolate. Beat until light and fluffy. Spoon mixture over crust. Place in the freezer.

Whip cream until soft peaks form. Fold marshmallows into whipped cream. Remove pan from freezer and spread marshmallow mixture over chocolate layer. Sprinkle with crushed candy. Freeze before serving, if you wish.

SERVES 9–12

THE PACKING HOUSE

900 E. Layton Avenue, Milwaukee
(414) 483-5054
packinghousemke.com
Owner: Margaret Wiken

Two things about The Packing House are unusual: It sits in the shadow of General Mitchell International Airport, and it has drive-through service twice a week.

The drive-through was added in the 1980s for the overflow of Friday fish fry orders. It is not unusual to see a four-block-long line of cars during Lenten season, when eight hundred to one thousand fish dinners are sold per week. During winter the range drops to five hundred to six hundred.

In 2014, drive-through service expanded to include fried chicken dinners on Tuesday (complete with mashed potatoes, gravy, green beans almondine, and a biscuit). Sometimes customers take their orders to the airport's outdoor observation area, less than one block away, for an aerial show of takeoffs and landings while dining.

You could say this supper club is where General Manager Chris Wiken got his roots and wings, in more than one way. Parents Keith and Margaret Wiken opened The Packing House in 1974, taking Chris there as a toddler to watch *Sesame Street* while they cleaned. Soon it was their son who was doing the work, and by the time he was fifteen, those paychecks were buying him flight lessons.

Chris earned a pilot's license by age sixteen, but bold initiatives didn't end there. Two years later, while still in high school, he was elected an alderman for the city of St. Francis, unseating the Common Council president on a campaign budget of around eighteen hundred dollars. "My dad always said 'find your calling, find your passion, and go for it,' which is what I try to do in life." He was studying pre-law at Marquette University when his father died in 1993.

"I was in my senior year, and I had to make a quick choice," Chris explains. If he wanted a role managing the family business, now was the time. That's what he did until 2001, but being next to Mitchell Field was a daily reminder of other possibilities. Chris took a chance on flying as a career, both as a flight instructor and commercial pilot. Getting hired by Aloha Airlines meant moving to Hawaii in 2004, but this wasn't about landing in paradise. When the airline filed for bankruptcy protection six months later, Chris found himself out of a job.

He returned to restaurant work because that's what he knew, and he found his way back to Milwaukee. Now he flies for the fun of it and finds value in customer service. "The personal sacrifices, long work hours, and passion we have for serving people" are worth it, Chris says, because "we are a part of family traditions, which I find very rewarding."

You know the saying: "What goes around comes around." The customers care, too. A woman from Racine, thirty miles south, says her lunch group meets here every Tuesday, in honor of a thirty-year Packing House bartender who died in 2013.

Jeff Stoll in 2015 marks thirty-five years of piano playing at the supper club; Rat Pack music is a specialty. Newer to the scene is executive chef Nick Scheeler, who gets credit for the restaurant's first menu overhaul in twenty years. "Modern twists to longtime favorites" is how Chris explains the changes. That includes introducing cheese and charcuterie plates, a veal chop entrée, and Gardener's Pie—a vegetarian version of the popular shepherd's pie.

Some things won't change, like the house-made banana cream pie; dozens are sold each week. "It's the clear dessert favorite—you probably could combine all the other choices and still have that as what sells the most," Chris says.

Chris Wiken calls this "our iconic and bestselling appetizer. Salty, savory, and sweet combine to create a dish that's both elegant and simple." Use canned water chestnuts. Keep the sauce warm while baking the bacon wraps.

BACON-WRAPPED WATER CHESTNUTS

Combine all sauce ingredients in a small saucepan. Place over low heat, stirring regularly. When sugars are completely dissolved and sauce is runny in consistency, remove from heat.

Preheat oven to 375°F. Drain and rinse water chestnuts. Cut bacon in half, creating shorter pieces that are even in length.

Wrap each half-slice of bacon around a water chestnut and affix with a toothpick.

Place on a cookie sheet (don't overlap) and bake 20 to 25 minutes, or until crispy and well browned. Arrange in serving bowl or on a platter. Rewarm reserved sauce and drizzle over the appetizer generously.

SERVES 6–12

For the sauce:
1 cup brown sugar
1 cup granulated sugar
½ cup soy sauce
½ cup water

For the wrapped bacon:
24 water chestnuts
12 slices thick bacon
12 toothpicks

Three miles from The Packing House is the factory whose products uphold Wisconsin's "Cheesehead" nickname. The wedge-shaped Cheesehead hat that Ralph Bruno invented in 1987 prevails on the heads of sports fans and others today.

The Foamation line of products also includes cheesy yellow foam cowboy hats, baseball hats, crowns, graduation caps, sombreros, tiaras, top hats, neckties, earrings, belt buckles, and purses. The company also takes custom orders, which means corn-shaped Huskerheads for Nebraska sports fans. cheesehead.com, (414) 481-3337

Both the bacon appetizer and this entree have stayed on The Packing House menu almost forty years. Unlike traditional chicken cordon bleu that is pan-fried, The Packing House relies on a tender puff pastry to create a more refined dish that in no way skimps on flavor. The result is a modified version of a universally recognized French classic, Chris says, "identifiable as distinctly ours." The chicken is topped with Champagne Mushroom Béchamel Sauce.

Chris acknowledges that this recipe takes a little time and patience to prepare. He has considered removing the entree from the dinner menu for these reasons, but there is one problem: Customers keep ordering it.

CHICKEN CORDON BLEU

For the chicken:

1 (6-ounce) ham steak, ⅜ inches thick

6 asparagus spears

6 (8-ounce) boneless, skinless chicken breasts

Salt, to taste

Pepper, to taste

1 tablespoon grated Parmesan cheese

12 slices swiss cheese

1 sheet puff pastry dough

2 eggs

For the sauce:

1 tablespoon butter

16 ounces button mushrooms, finely sliced

1 shallot, finely diced

1 garlic clove, finely minced

1 tablespoon flour

1 cup chicken broth

Pinch of white pepper

3 sprigs fresh thyme

6 ounces dry Champagne

½ cup heavy cream

Preheat oven to 450°F. Cut ham steak into six roughly even batons. Cut asparagus spears in half.

Pound out chicken breasts with a meat hammer between two sheets of plastic wrap until uniformly ¼ inch thick. Sprinkle bone side of chicken breast liberally with salt, pepper, and Parmesan cheese.

Place two slices of swiss cheese on each chicken breast, overlapping slices slightly. Place 1 piece ham and 2 pieces asparagus about one third of the way from the tail (tapered) end of each chicken breast.

Roll up each chicken breast, beginning at the tail end. Place in roasting pan, seam side down. Fill pan ¼ inch deep with water. Bake 18 minutes. Remove rolled chicken and chill thoroughly.

Thaw puff pastry sheet and cut into 6 square-like pieces. Wrap each cooled chicken breast in puff dough, tucking under corners as needed to create a smooth appearance on top.

Whip the eggs in small bowl and brush over wrapped chicken.

Bake on a greased cookie sheet at 450°F for 15 minutes, until chicken is thoroughly cooked and puff pastry shell is golden brown.

As chicken bakes, make the sauce. Melt the butter in a large saucepan. Before butter browns, add mushrooms, shallots, and garlic. Sauté 5 to 8 minutes, until mushrooms are thoroughly cooked.

Add flour and stir constantly, until fully incorporated. Slowly stir in chicken broth. Add pepper and thyme. Bring to a boil.

Add Champagne and heavy cream. Simmer about 10 minutes. Serve sauce hot with chicken.

SERVES 6

RED CIRCLE INN AND BISTRO

N44 W33013 Watertown Plank Road, Nashotah
(262) 367-4883
redcircleinn.com
Owners: Martha and Norm Eckstaedt

Wisconsin's oldest restaurant opened in 1848 as a stagecoach stop, and within ten years a railroad stop was added one block away. Both made the Nashotah Hotel a popular destination for travelers, especially when summer getaways on nearby lakes were built for the Milwaukee area's richest families.

Beer baron Frederick Pabst was among the fans, and when he bought the hotel in 1889, he called it the Red Circle Inn, a name that matched the logo of his burgeoning brewery. Although the Pabst family only kept the property until 1911, the name endures and relatives of the successors—longtime Pabst employee Steven Polaski and wife Hulda—would maintain ownership for four generations.

All of this makes the Red Circle much more than a business venture to the Eckstaedts, who assumed ownership in 1993. "It's a tremendous responsibility

to keep perpetrating this history," Norm says. "We may own the place, but we're just the caretakers." Coincidentally, the Red Circle was the first place he worked (as an assistant manager) after college graduation in 1980.

Despite the boom in attention because of new transportation routes in the 1800s, Nashotah is a small town of fourteen hundred residents today and is thirty miles west of Milwaukee. The private location has made it a prime site for historic moments. One example: Major League Baseball owners in the 1950s met here when deciding to move the Braves from Boston to Milwaukee.

A couple of other Wisconsin restaurateurs bristle when the Red Circle is described as the state's oldest restaurant, but Norm is neither surprised nor concerned. He says he has seen the original land grant for the property, on file

at the Waukesha County Clerk's office. On his supper club's walls are enlarged photos from the years of Polaski family ownership. An ornate wooden bar, brought over from Austria by the Pabst family in 1889, anchors an upstairs banquet room. On the face of dinner plates are the words "Wisconsin's oldest restaurant."

Much has been remodeled inside and out at the dinner-only restaurant, whose executive chef is James Brown. "You have to evolve," Norm says, but "there's a resurgence back to classic dishes." Beef Wellington might be the most popular menu entree, but the Red Circle also offers no less than six choices of fresh fish per night. In the bar is a bistro menu of small-plate portions of beef or seafood Wellington, veal sweetbreads, strip loin sliders, and other bites of delicately prepared gourmet fare.

"About the only thing we don't make is bread," Norm says. "Our stock is made from scratch, our soufflés are made to order. We even make Thousand Island dressing, although not many people order it anymore." Subtle influences include the Bon Bree cheese from Williams Homestead Creamery, less than twenty miles southeast of the Red Circle. The firm cows' milk cheese with a creamy taste tops the french onion soup, Norm says, because of its taste and "it melts perfectly."

When frog legs are on a Wisconsin supper club menu today, they likely are simply pan-fried or breaded and deep-fried, like chicken. This recipe hails from Southern France, where frog legs remain popular on restaurant menus.

"It's pretty basic—not too complicated," Norm says. "I think you'll see that this preparation is classic and still embraced in France" for frog legs. One pound of frog legs equals about three saddles, or six legs.

Note that a final recipe step involves the licorice-flavored Pernod. Ouzo is similar in flavor, easier to find, and cheaper, but Norm does not recommend using it because the sugar content is higher.

FROG LEGS PROVENÇAL

1 pound frog legs
Salt, to taste
White pepper, to taste
½ cup flour
2 tablespoons clarified butter
2 cloves garlic, minced
¼ cup sliced scallions
2 tablespoons chopped parsley
½ cup diced tomatoes
½ cup dry white wine
¾ ounce Pernod

Pat dry the frog legs. Season with salt and white pepper. Lightly coat the entire leg with flour.

Melt butter in large sauté pan over medium heat. Sauté the frog legs 2 to 3 minutes on each side, or until golden brown. Add garlic (do not let it burn), and 1 minute later add scallions, parsley, and diced tomatoes. Sauté all ingredients for 1 more minute.

Remove frog legs from pan and keep warm. Deglaze pan with white wine and reduce sauce for another minute or two. Flame with Pernod.

Serve sauce over frog legs and a bed of angel-hair pasta, couscous, or rice.

SERVES 2

Here is another longtime recipe that Norm says was especially popular in the 1970s. "Few restaurants do it anymore because fewer places serve veal," he observes. "It's popular here because people know we do it," and Veal Holstein was on the Red Circle Inn menu long before the Eckstaedts bought the supper club. Buy the scaloppine from your local butcher, he advises.

VEAL HOLSTEIN

Delicately season the veal with salt and pepper. Dredge each piece of meat in flour. Dip into the egg wash (1 beaten egg). Coat with bread crumbs.

Melt butter in large sauté pan over medium heat. Sauté four scaloppine 2 to 3 minutes on each side, or until golden brown. Move meat to a wire rack and hold in a 275°F oven. Repeat the process for the remaining veal.

Individually sauté 2 eggs over easy, being certain to not overcook the yolks.

Place veal onto two plates. Top each serving with an egg and then crisscross anchovy fillets over each egg. Sprinkle capers atop all. Serve with small dumplings (spaetzle), creamy herbed whipped potatoes, or lyonnaise potatoes.

SERVES 2

8 scaloppine of veal (about 12 ounces)
Salt, to taste
Pepper, to taste
½ cup flour
1 beaten egg
½ cup bread crumbs
Clarified butter, as needed
2 eggs
4 anchovy fillets
2 tablespoons capers

SMOKY'S CLUB

3005 University Avenue, Madison
(608) 233-2120
smokysclub.com
Owners: Tom and Larry Schmock

Customers for decades have felt compelled to leave their mark at Smoky's, thanks to Janet Schmock's habit of accumulating glitz, kitsch, and critters for decor. In that latter category were plastic lobsters, stuffed toy alligators, and a huge muskie reeled in by her husband, Leonard.

University of Wisconsin Badger football fans tucked game tickets into ceiling tiles. Dormant wasp nests, wineskins, cowbells, birdless cages, Smokey Bears, sports pennants, and much more found a home here. Soon the critters were wearing silk ties and other accessories. The Schmocks even found a place for a customer's golf clubs, and their son's own untapped birthday piñata hung from rafters almost forty years.

"It was garage-sale-esque, but I liked it," says son Larry. He and brother Tom have owned Smoky's since 1999. "People would want to be a part of the place," and "it was almost like we were Wall Drug" in South Dakota, after Internet access made more and more curious travelers aware of the supper club.

So much hung from the ceiling that the tiles started to buckle, and the brothers removed about two thirds of the paraphernalia when the ceiling was replaced in 2010. Among the survivors are a mounted marlin, a dried blowfish, and a sign that says that profanity is not tolerated. Sports artifacts include a framed autographed photo of Elroy "Crazylegs" Hirsch, a 1968 NFL Hall of Fame running back and receiver who got his start on the University of Wisconsin team.

Crazylegs was a Saturday night regular at Smoky's until he died in 2004, and as a teen he washed dishes at Justo's Club, which is where Smoky's now stands. Leonard and Janet Schmock opened their first version of the restaurant in 1953, one block away, and moved into Justo's sixteen years later because the widening of University Avenue to four lanes forced them out. The original Smoky's was torn down, and the present location doubled in size in the 1980s, so at least 120 can dine at one time today.

"We're more of a hybrid supper club because we're a steakhouse too," Tom says. Good cooks know that the secret to excellence in steak is a nice fast sear. At Smoky's, that happens at four hundred degrees on a thick, flat steel grill that holds the heat. "You can't reproduce a seasoned grill like this at home," he maintains. "That's the only way to go—it doesn't matter what the cut (of meat) is."

The arrival to Madison of steakhouses that are national chains—Fleming's, Ruth's Chris—challenges places like Smoky's but don't redefine it. "Comfy, eclectic, and homey" is how Larry describes the place. "Being able to bring back a spark of memory—that's our ace in the hole."

The brothers like seeing one generation of customers grow into a second and third. They witness life passages, big and small. That includes kids allowed to order their first steak, kind of a rite of passage into manhood, as Larry sees it.

The neighborhood also has not been immune to notorious characters. Bar-grill operator Jennie Justo, nicknamed "Queen of the Bootleggers," was sentenced in 1931 to a year in jail for operating a speakeasy. Customers loyal to Smoky's included jet-setter Marion Roberts; he pleaded guilty in 1971 to tax evasion, after a federal grand jury indictment.

It all made life interesting for Janet and Leonard, who met while working at the same restaurant. She was a farm girl, the youngest of ten kids, who moved to Madison at age seventeen to work as a nanny, housekeeper, and cook for well-off families. He was a Navy pilot who worked as a crop duster after World

War II. That's how he earned the nickname "Smoky." "Twice he had to climb out of a tree" when the crop dusting went awry, Larry says, and that was a contributing factor in his father's decision to seek another line of work.

The Schmock boys, without a hint of regret, say they seemed born to take over their parents' business. Both sons were raised in the restaurant's upstairs apartment and were automatically treated like family by salesmen, deliverymen, customers, and staff. "I was a salad girl and filling beer coolers at age six," Larry deadpans. "We never intended to do anything else" as a career.

Employees become family, some stay for a lifetime or—as Larry puts it—"they don't leave until we bury them. Rose, Betty, and Jane are among the few who retired first."

Longtimers include "Martini Bob" Perry, a mixologist who has worked behind Smoky's bar since 1980. Wife Cindy, who has greeted customers since 1983, gets a clear view of his antics. Martinis come in two sizes (ten- and five-ounce), and Martini Bob has concocted hundreds of cocktail recipes, some listed at martinibobs.com. In his repertoire are at least one dozen unusual ice-cream drinks, in addition to the grasshopper and other classics.

"Those drinks are meant to be shared," Martini Bob says. "Some couples come here late at night, to do just that." Others come with new cocktail ideas for the bartender, who is glad to experiment and enroll them in Martini Bob's Martini Club. Membership has earned at least twenty-three hundred people a certificate suitable for framing and the chance of adding their name to the docket of cocktails.

One of the more recent recipes was named after a group of women who called themselves the Outlaws, so that also is the name of the drink, a combo of Apple Pucker, honey whiskey, brandy, cinnamon, and lime juice. Although much of the eclectic decorating is gone from Smoky's, the martini club gives customers another way to leave their mark on the place.

The Schmock brothers since 1995 are co-owners of The Blue Moon Bar and Grill in Madison, known for its burger and craft beer selections. The location, near Camp Randall Stadium, is closer to the University of Wisconsin campus than Smoky's Club.

The lively, two-level brewpub has art deco decor. With the Blue Moon burger and chicken sandwich come raw onions and garlic blue cheese. "When somebody tells us Smoky's should be open for lunch, we tell them to go there," Larry Schmock says. What's behind the name? "Every once in a blue moon you enter a bar and grill that offers something to entice everyone," bluemoonbar.com explains.

The third Schmock sibling, Barbara Schmock, is a registered nurse who also is known for the cookies that she sells at Badger football games and beyond. She bakes them in the kitchen of Smoky's Club.

"Martini Bob" Perry named this drink after Oscar Mayer, who made his Madison meat-processing plant the headquarters for Oscar Mayer & Co. until it was moved to Chicago in 1955. Martini Bob's dad worked at the Oscar Mayer plant for thirty years. The cocktail turns into a relish tray in a glass because the bartender adds a fat assortment of garnishes: stalks of celery and asparagus, a dill pickle wedge, a cherry tomato, plain and garlic-stuffed olives, a pickled green bean, and slices of summer sausage, cucumber, and lime. A-1 is the bartender's preferred steak sauce, and he dips the martini glass rim into a zesty Johnny Velvet Spice Mix, produced locally and sold through johnnyvelvet. com. Note: Instead of buying bacon-infused vodka, you can make your own by adding 1 tablespoon melted bacon fat to 12 ounces of unflavored vodka. Shake, let the mixture infuse a few hours, and place in the refrigerator until the fat rises to the top. Strain through cheesecloth.

BLOODY OSCAR

1 dill pickle spear
4 ounces Bloody Mary mix
2 ounces bacon-infused vodka
Dash of steak sauce
Dash of Worcestershire sauce
Pinch of basil

Flash blend pickle spear, Bloody Mary mix, and one or two handfuls of ice. Add remaining ingredients and mix well. Serve straight up in a frosted martini glass with your choice of garnishes.

SERVES 1

This is one of supper club founder Janet Schmock's much-loved recipes from the 1950s, and for a long time it was served as a complimentary treat to dinner guests. Now it is a side dish option.

BLENDED COTTAGE CHEESE

Mix cottage cheese, caraway seeds, and pepper in a large bowl. Dice green onions and mix with remaining ingredients.

Refrigerate overnight to 24 hours before serving to enhance flavor.

MAKES 1 QUART

2 (16-ounce) containers small-curd cottage cheese
2 tablespoons caraway seeds
1 tablespoon pepper
6 green onions

TOBY'S SUPPER CLUB

3717 S. Dutch Mill Road, Madison
(608) 222-6913
tobyssupperclub.com
Owner: Roxanne Peterson

George and Judy Thorson moved to Wisconsin from Spokane, Washington, in the 1950s, after the end of his stint as a military police officer for the Air Force. Daughter Roxanne was four years old and about to begin a lifelong attachment to the area.

Her parents built a house on her grandparents' farm, and no more than half a mile down the road was a supper club that Toby and Lila Curtis had owned since 1941. The building started as a barbershop, with a little bootlegging on the side during Prohibition. Roxanne says her grandfather was among the people who quietly operated a still and sold his hooch there.

Her mother began working one shift per week at Toby's, the supper club, waitressing and washing dishes. Roxanne's first meal there was a kiddie cocktail and shrimp ("I didn't like either one"). The area, at that time rural Dane County, today is a slow sprawl that eventually will link Madison to McFarland.

After Toby Curtis died in 1960, the supper club went up for sale. The Thorsons bought Toby's nine years later, even though they had never operated a restaurant in their lives. They didn't change the name because the restaurant already was well-known, and they didn't want to rock that boat.

"They looked at it as the makings for a good life," Roxanne says, to explain why her parents made the bold move. Dinner service lasted six hours, until 11:30 nightly, to give farm families time to finish fieldwork and cow milking, but others came, too. "Every night, we were kicking people out of here—they'd play the juke box, dance, and go to each other's houses for breakfast."

When the restaurant expanded in 1972, in the wall was an original menu (thirty-five cents for a perch plate, $1.95 for a sixteen-ounce T-bone steak), newspaper clippings, gin bottles from Prohibition, and more.

Roxanne took over ownership in 1991, after her father died, but it's more complicated than that. Her work as the manager of Toby's began in 1972 because of the parent's ongoing health challenges. That's the same year she began work as a hospital registered nurse, a career she has retained, except for an eight-year leave to tend to other matters.

That means she usually shows up around 4 a.m. to pay bills, place food/supply orders, and bake the cinnamon rolls that go on the tables for lunch, Monday through Thursday. Toby's began serving lunch in 2010 because customers asked for it; the restaurant parking lot is nearly full on an average weekday. Food service ends promptly at 2 p.m. and resumes three hours later.

Nine of twenty employees are Roxanne's relatives; that includes her two children, Chris Wilson and Kelly Gill. Sister Rhonda Frank is a waitress, described as "stellar." The crew, in some ways, is interchangeable because of their knowledge about each other's jobs. They make french dressing by the gallon, in addition to from-scratch Thousand Island, a vinaigrette, and blue cheese

in smaller batches. One of the secret ingredients in honey-mustard dressing is a ranch dressing mix.

A while back the kitchen would grind hundreds of pounds of potatoes by hand, for hash browns fried in the same cast-iron skillets that Lila Curtis owned. Those skillets are still used today. "We know the recipes by heart," Roxanne says, with the exception of nephew Tony Dalbec's secret and well-received Key Lime Pie Martini. "A lot have gotten drunk trying to figure it out. I hope he gets rich off the recipe."

Tony is pretty much in charge of the dessert bar, too, because the only offerings involve ice cream. That's because most customers are too full for dessert after eating steaks, pan-fried chicken, or seafood. People with a sweet tooth can order vanilla ice cream with chocolate sauce or one of Tony's hefty ice-cream drinks.

Own an "Official" Toby's Can Coozie only #2⁰⁰

Customers, as always, are a mix of white and blue collars, people who represent diverse walks of life. They hang out with a cocktail (Roxanne says drinks with brandy outnumber those with whiskey, 5 to 1) at the circular bar, where a waitress shows up to take food orders, then guides them to a table when it's ready. That wait might be more than an hour, but few seem to care because of the friendly and ongoing banter among strangers.

Roxanne recalls the arrival of a busload of young adults, on a supper club tour and savoring one course per stop. They were dressed in poodle skirts and saddle shoes, 1950s attire, and living up their new-to-us dining experience. "I guess everybody wants to get on the supper club bandwagon," she says.

Toby's is known for its hash brown potatoes, and the recipe was passed down from the family who operated the supper club from 1941 to 1969. "Modern times and more customer demand have brought changes," Roxanne offers. "Now we shred the potatoes with a food grinder."

Just as important as the ingredients is the skillet. "That's the real secret," Roxanne says. "We use cast-iron, seasoned skillets that have never seen anything but hash browns. They were passed to us from the previous owners—making those skillets over sixty years old."

PERFECT SUPPER CLUB HASH BROWNS

2 pounds baby red potatoes
2 tablespoons butter-flavored oil
Salt, to taste
Pepper, to taste
Onions, optional
Shredded cheese, optional

Boil potatoes until tender. Chill. Peel, slice, and chop by hand.

Heat oil in a skillet. Add potatoes. Season with salt and pepper. Cook 10 to 12 minutes, or until golden brown on both sides, flipping at the halfway mark.

If adding onions, sauté in oil until soft before adding potatoes.

Cheese, if desired, tops the potatoes at the end of sautéing. Briefly cover pan to melt the cheese.

SERVES 4

Original cream drinks were made with heavy cream poured over ice, Roxanne notes, and ice cream became a popular addition to these after-dinner cocktails in the early 1960s.

She counts the pretty Pink Squirrel among the quintessential ice-cream drinks. The red and almond-flavored crème de noyaux is what gives the cocktail its pink color. "Modern times have brought back the use of heavy cream" instead of ice cream, Roxanne says, and these cocktails are shaken and served up in a martini glass.

PINK SQUIRREL

1 ounce crème de noyaux
1 ounce white crème de cacao
3 scoops vanilla ice cream
Maraschino cherry

Blend or whip by hand the first three ingredients. Pour into a serving glass. Garnish with cherry.

SERVES 1–2

acknowledgments

Many people and resources helped make this book possible. I especially appreciate:

The prolific author and good-humored Martin Hintz of Milwaukee. He recommended that Globe Pequot take a chance on me.

Tracy Kosbau, Kate Reiser, and Ed Lump of the Wisconsin Restaurant Association. Their magazine assignments deepen my understanding of food trends and the restaurant industry. Their observations and reference materials for this project were extremely helpful.

My friend Terese Allen, a long-respected food activist and food historian in Wisconsin. Her enthusiastic and encyclopedic knowledge of the state's food and foodways are on-target and insightful.

Therese Oldenburg, who initiated wisconsinsupperclubs.net. Her non-profit effort rounds up supper clubs and promotes them as one entity.

Nick Hoffman, curator at the History Museum at the Castle, Appleton. Supper clubs were a pertinent segment of his "Food: Who We Are and What We Eat" exhibit.

Holly De Ruyter, whose 2015 documentary *Old Fashioned: The Story of the Wisconsin Supper Club* adds history and insight to why we embrace supper club dining in the Badger State.

Ron Faiola, creator of *Wisconsin Supper Clubs: An Old Fashioned Experience*, a 2013 book and 2011 documentary. Both beautifully depict some of the players who keep this culinary heritage alive and sparked a revival of interest in supper club dining.

Photographers for Mark's East Side in Appleton (pages xvii, 104), The Aberdeen near Manitowish Waters (page 7), Calderwood Lodge near Luck (page 12), Mr. G's in Jacksonport (pages 36, 38), Food Fight (page 135), Dorf Haus in Roxbury (page 157), The Packing House (pages 190 and top of 192), Smoky's Club (page 206), and Joey Gerard's (top right cover photo) in Mequon. Their good works complement my own.

The supper club operators. Many dug through scrapbooks and albums for many priceless, vintage photos of their businesses.

Fans of my weekly "Roads Traveled" columns, syndicated since 2002. They are my reality check in many ways.

My longtime partner, Dick Franken, and the many friends who helped taste test all of these recipes.

Most important: my editor Tracee Williams. Her enthusiasm, patience, and steady navigation are what every writer needs.

INDEX OF SUPPER CLUBS

INDEX

About the Author

Midwest travel, regional foods, German heritage, and environmental sustainability are Mary Bergin's writing specialties. The lifelong professional journalist boasts decades of newspaper work as an editor and reporter in Wisconsin, Indiana, Kentucky, and Oklahoma. Her weekly syndicated and award-winning "Roads Traveled" column began in 2002.

The *Chicago Tribune* frequently publishes Mary's work in its travel section. Wisconsin Public Radio counts her among its travel experts. Her freelance work is a featured case study in the college textbook *Travel Journalism: On the Road with Serious Intent* by Professor John F. Greenman at the University of Georgia.

Mary is a Wisconsin native who grew up on a farm and lives in Madison. *The Wisconsin Supper Club Cookbook* is her fifth book. She is a member of the Society of American Travel Writers, Association of Food Journalists, and Midwest Travel Writers Association. Learn more about her and the Midwest at marybergin.com and roadstraveled.com.